BUILD YOUR OWN
CARPORT & PERGOLA

ACKNOWLEDGEMENTS

The authors and publishers wish to acknowledge the many people who helped to compile this book. Many shared their time and expertise, while others contributed by allowing us to photograph structures in their gardens, or feature their designs. We thank Mike Ingram, regional director of Corobrik, Western Cape, whose advice on brickwork proved invaluable; Jock Lamb for sharing his brick-paving skills in the step-by-step paving project; Fanie le Roux and Nick Irish, group merchandising director of Federated Timbers and Simon Clarke of Mitek for assistance with the step-by-step carport; Lindsay Weyer, marketing manager of Alnet, who made the pergola project possible; and the Desmond Crowie Construction Company, especially Tony Crowie, for help with the step-by-step project on throwing a concrete slab. Thanks also to Brian Mollagrean who appears in the photographs of the concrete work project, and George Wenman, who posed for the pergola project.

Several people checked part or all of the completed manuscript for accuracy. We are especially grateful to Steve Crosswell, regional director of the Portland Cement Institute, Western Cape, who read the entire text. Also to Colin Kalis of Ready Mix Concrete, who verified concrete specifications and quantities; Ian Seymour of Seymour Paving for help with the paving sections; Lewis Silberbauer, technical manager of Mondi Timbers, for checking and advising on wood.

A special thank-you to the people who allowed us to use their carports and pergolas in the Designs and Plans section. Some were professionally designed, others were erected by contractors, while a couple were DIY projects. Designers include Henk van't Hof (5 and 6), Jacqueline Cole (8), and architect Alison Standish (9 and 11). Both the DIY structures (4 and 7) were designed and built by Janek Szymanowski.

We also acknowledge the assistance of Wardkiss Homecare which so kindly loaned tools for photography.

Finally we thank the other people who were involved in the often laborious behind-the-scenes production of the book itself. In particular, editor Jenny Barrett, project coordinator Annlerie van Rooyen, designer Lauren Mendelson, and illustrator Henk van't Hof.

Struik Publishers (Pty) Ltd
(a member of The Struik Publishing Group (Pty) Ltd)
Cornelis Struik House
80 McKenzie Street
Cape Town 8001

Reg. No.: 54/00965/07

First published by Struik Publishers (Pty) Ltd in 1994

Text © Penny Swift 1994
Photographs © Janek Szymanowski 1994
Illustrations © Penny Swift and Janek Szymanowski 1994

Editor Jenny Barrett
Project coordinator Annlerie van Rooyen
Designer and cover designer Lauren Mendelson
Assistant designer Lellyn Creamer
Photographer Janek Szymanowski
Illustrator Henk van't Hof
Proofreader and indexer Sandie Vahl

Typesetting by Struik DTP, Cape Town
Reproduction by Unifoto (Pty) Ltd, Cape Town
Printed and bound by Tien Wah Press (Pte) Ltd, Singapore

ISBN 1 86825 543 3

All rights reserved. No part of this publication may be reproduced, stored in a retrieval system or transmitted, in any form or by any means, electronic, mechanical, photocopying, recording or otherwise, without the prior written permission of the copyright holders and publishers.

Also available in Afrikaans as *Bou Jou Eie Motorafdak en Prieel*

The information in this book is true and complete to the best of our knowledge. All recommendations are made without guarantee on the part of the authors and the publishers. The authors and publishers disclaim any liability for damages resulting from the use of this information.

CONTENTS

INTRODUCTION	**6**
PLANNING	**8**
Building regulations	11
The role of the professional	13
DESIGN AND STYLE	**14**
Historical perspective	15
Choosing climbers and creepers	23
Security	25
CONSTRUCTION PRINCIPLES	**28**
Setting out	31
Special connectors for poles	36
STEP-BY-STEP GUIDE TO CONCRETE WORK	**42**
STEP-BY-STEP GUIDE TO BRICK PAVING	**44**
STEP-BY-STEP GUIDE TO BUILDING A CARPORT	**46**
STEP-BY-STEP GUIDE TO BUILDING A PERGOLA	**48**
DESIGNS AND PLANS	**52**
Plan 1: Wood on wood	52
Plan 2: Popular precast	53
Plan 3: Carport for shade	54
Plan 4: Simply single	55
Plan 5: Slate sophistication	56
Plan 6: Clever combination	57
Plan 7: Easy pole pergola	58
Plan 8: Precast perfection	59
Plan 9: Cut-wood creation	60
Plan 10: Period-style pergola	61
Plan 11: Porch pergola	62
Plan 12: Garden gazebo	63
INDEX	**64**
USEFUL ADDRESSES	**64**

INTRODUCTION

Structures of various types are found in gardens all over the world, and have been for centuries. In fact very few gardens are without some feature which offers shelter or screening, or which simply adds a decorative quality.

Since the earliest times pergolas, overhead beams, arches and arbours have been constructed to support vines and other climbing plants. Sometimes the fruits from the plants were of primary importance, but more frequently, the structure was built to give shade from the sun.

While many structures are still erected to support climbing plants or to create a secluded area where one can sit, there is much more emphasis these days on practicality.

Over the years the terminology has become somewhat jumbled, with 'pergola', 'arbour' and 'overhead' all relating to a range of similar shelters built from a variety of materials (see page 15).

Perhaps the simplest of all these structures is the roofless pergola, which may be little more than a row of wooden poles supporting a series of crossbeams. At the other end of the scale is the gazebo (popular during the Victorian era), which can be quite simple or marvellously elaborate, practical or whimsical, the design depending on your taste and the style of your garden as a whole. There are also traditional arbours, typically designed to create a feeling of intimacy and seclusion in the garden.

One of the most common outdoor structures these days is the kind which is built adjacent to the house, and which is intended to extend the living area of the house both visually and in practical terms. It is frequently supported by at least one wall and is constructed to define an area for sitting or entertaining, effectively turning the space into an outdoor room. Poles, posts or pillars support beams (fixed to the existing brickwork), which in turn usually support a series of crosspieces or purlins.

Similar structures are often erected away from the house, and can be either freestanding or attached to a garden wall or outbuilding. These can be part of an area for entertaining or recreation, and feature a barbecue, built-in seating or a swimming pool. They may also be built to shade a walkway or driveway, or as a visual link between the house and the garden or patio.

To a lesser extent, pergolas are erected in the garden purely to add visual interest. While creepers and cascading, flowering plants will add a charming decorative quality to a pergola, it can look even more attractive when framing a statue or water feature. This approach should not be underestimated; even the simplest pergola, imaginatively constructed, can become a focal point and add a touch of romanticism to the most ordinary of gardens. With a canopy of plants, it will provide an intimate shelter and help create a feeling of seclusion.

Closely related to the pergola is the carport, a structure which has been developed for purely practical

A charming, period-style gazebo provides a perfect retreat in a suburban garden.

purposes. Carports are often built as a result of limited space or budget, and because many houses are now constructed without garages. In addition, because of escalating building costs, those people who do have garages often convert them to provide room for storage or extra living space. This has resulted in a marked increase in the popularity of carports as an easy alternative site for parking cars, caravans and even boats.

Adding a carport is certainly a simple, effective and relatively inexpensive home improvement project. There is no reason, however, for it to lack style and composition. All aspects of design which relate to other structures apply to the carport. It must be large enough to house one or more cars, and its design should be consistent with both the architecture of the house and the garden design. Whatever your needs, *Build Your Own Carport and Pergola* will help you to design and build a structure which suits the mood and style of your house and garden.

The first section contains some imaginative ideas and sound practical advice for all aspects of your project, from the planning stage right through to construction. Style is considered in relation to existing architectural features, as well as in the context of garden design. Suitable locations where you can build your carport or pergola are suggested, and details are given of materials which you can use not only for the basic structure, but also for the floor surface, roofing and screening. All relevant tools, materials and construction principles are discussed and illustrated, and some easy methods of quantifying and costing the various materials are described.

There is some fascinating information on the history of pergolas and similar structures, advice on choosing the best plants to enhance your pergola or carport, as well as a host of colour photographs to inspire you.

In the latter part of the book, we help you tackle the work with detailed step-by-step photographs. Project plans are also offered as examples, together with a checklist of materials required for each job. In most cases, formal building plans will have to be drawn up, although you could simply adapt the plans in this book to suit your property and location. The designs range from a very simple pergola structure built from poles, to complex carports incorporating concealed gutters, solid roofs and even additional storage areas. However, all of the projects are well within the capabilities of most DIY enthusiasts and home builders.

Even if you decide to employ someone else to do the work for you, *Build Your Own Carport and Pergola* is an invaluable guide which will inspire you and enable you to check that the job is being done properly.

An unusual pergola erected over a walkway adds interest to an entrance.

Pot plants flourish under a pergola.

A simple structure designed to shelter cars.

PLANNING

The decision to build a pergola, carport or other permanent structure in the garden requires a good deal of thought and planning. You should assess your needs carefully, as they will have a bearing on the functions the structure will fulfil, its appearance, size and position. Your design should also be chosen carefully to match the style of your house and garden. Costing the project is another important stage in planning your structure, especially for people working within a limited budget. If you plan thoroughly from the start, construction should run smoothly, resulting in a pleasing structure which will enhance the property.

YOUR NEEDS

A golden rule when building anything of a permanent nature is to ensure that it fulfils the function for which it has been built. All too often we duplicate features we have seen elsewhere, without considering our needs.

For instance, if your motivation for constructing a carport is to protect your car from the elements, it is essential to use long-lasting materials that will not only withstand weathering but also cut out the sun's harmful UV rays and shield the car from rain, hail and snow. If the structure is to shelter an outdoor area for entertaining, you will probably have to screen at least one side and consider overhead cover. On the other hand, a pergola erected primarily as a support for plants does not require a solid roof, and must only be strong enough to take the weight of the plants (see page 23).

The function the structure is intended to fulfil is crucial in determining the design and materials you use, and also has a direct bearing on where you will locate it.

FUNCTION

In hot climates, a pergola is useful for providing shade, since it can be designed to cover just about any space you wish. Planted with climbers, it will filter light and add intimacy and charm to the outdoor area.

Even in cooler climes, this type of structure can be immensely useful for sheltering a patio or terrace. Built alongside the house and topped with a fairly solid roofing material, a pergola can provide you with additional living space in most conditions, offering protection from the sun and rain. Constructed in the garden and covered with sweet-smelling plants, it can be the perfect place for weekend entertaining or simply a retreat for solitude.

A pergola may also be erected to shelter a walkway, leading through the garden or to the entrance of the house, or to shade a water feature. Its primary function may even be to provide privacy – a common motivating factor in densely populated areas, where small plots are often overlooked by neighbours.

Similarly, a carport is designed to give shelter to vehicles and the people using them. However, like any structure, it requires an appropriate roof if it is to shield the parking area from the elements effectively.

You may, of course, be planning a carport or pergola simply to create interest – to improve the aesthetic appeal of the exterior of your house, to add another dimension to your garden, or simply to define the area where cars should park. In some cases, a carport will have no distinct parking surface and no roof, but it will still demarcate an acceptable home base for cars.

Once you have established what your needs and preferences are, and the primary function your structure will fulfil, you will be able to determine exactly what to build.

SITE

Having decided on the type of structure you need, you will probably know exactly where your pergola or carport should be sited. However, there are factors which should be considered before you start building. Accessibility, for example, must be carefully planned, especially when the structure is built primarily for practical reasons. As it is permanent, you cannot afford to make a mistake.

A retractable canvas awning gives welcome shade whenever necessary.

8 BUILD YOUR OWN CARPORT AND PERGOLA

A pergola which will give shelter to an alfresco dining area will probably be sited near the house, possibly adjacent to the living room or kitchen. If a barbecue is incorporated into the patio design, it may well be sited further away from the dwelling because of the problem of smoke. More often than not, a traditional arbour is tucked away in a private section of the garden, or is set at the end of a walkway. Alternatively, it may be sited at the junction of two intersecting pathways – in a formal rose garden, for instance.

There is often one obvious site for a carport – in front of or alongside the garage, or adjacent to the front entrance of the house – but this is not always the case. If there is more than one option, consider the advantages and disadvantages of each, focusing on the question of accessibility. A carport built any distance from the house may give vehicles protection on rainy days, but it certainly will not keep the occupants dry as they dash for the front door. If you live in a high rainfall area, consider incorporating a covered walkway from the carport to the house. This may simply mean extending the carport roof covering to the front door, or it may require the erection of an additional structure.

While the dimensions of pergolas are of course variable, carports are designed specifically for vehicles, and must therefore house them adequately. There must be enough space for car doors to be opened and for passengers to move in and out comfortably. A carport large enough in terms of both floor area and height for a station-wagon or caravan, for example, could increase the resale value of your property. However, make sure that the site you choose can accommodate the proportions required.

One of the most common mistakes made by over-zealous do-it-yourselfers is not taking the house and garden plan into consideration. All too often the result is a structure which looks as though it is an afterthought. You can avoid this by considering the property as a whole, ensuring that architectural

A pretty pergola adds character to the façade of a gracious, thatched home.

Alfresco meals are a treat on this vine-covered patio.

BUILD YOUR OWN CARPORT AND PERGOLA 9

styles match, that existing features and those which you are planning will complement each other, and that the position you have chosen will enable you to create a harmonious whole.

Even if an expert is constructing the carport or pergola for you (see page 13), it is a good idea to draw a scale plan of the whole property, indicating all planting and structures, however big or small. The easiest way to do this is on ordinary graph paper, using a simple measurement which relates to the number of squares on the sheet. If necessary, join two sheets together. Alternatively, obtain a copy of your house plans from the local council, and enlarge the relevant area with the aid of graph paper or a photocopier.

With a scale drawing to hand, you can start to visualise what the finished product will look like, and whether, in fact, the pergola or carport fits into the alotted space. If there are several possible sites, cut out templates of your structure and any additional features, and shift them about on the piece of paper until you are sure of the best option.

When planning to locate the structure alongside the house, make sure that it will not make nearby rooms too dark. If there are trees and shrubs nearby, ascertain whether they will affect the structure. Any trees that must be felled

This pergola, built of poles, will eventually have a covering of climbing plants.

or overhanging branches that must be removed should be dealt with before building begins, to prevent damage to the structure at a later stage.

Before finalising your choice of site, inspect the ground on which you plan to build. Is it sound, or will additional foundations be necessary? If the land slopes, are retaining walls required?

Do you have to cut into a bank and remove soil; or will you need extra fill to help level the site?

MATERIALS

The materials chosen for any pergola or carport will be determined largely by the function you intend it to have and the style you choose, although cost, of course, is often an important factor (see page 12). At the same time, it is important that they match or complement the house and its architectural style, as well as other features and elements in the garden such as boundary walls and paving.

Take care to ensure that the proportions of beams and uprights are in keeping with both the structure and the garden as a whole. If beams are undersized, for instance, they will appear flimsy and the structure will seem to be taller than it really is.

All structures should obviously be sound and long-lasting. While the traditional arbour is fashioned from soft stems which will eventually decay, leaving the plants to form a permanent cover (see page 15), pergolas,

A relatively plain pergola defines a patio built alongside a house.

BUILDING REGULATIONS

Building regulations are designed to set minimum standards for all construction work. Many of them address safety issues, to ensure that structures are sound and will not collapse, even in the most adverse conditions. Related codes also specify standards for materials and, in some instances, techniques used for building. Another major concern of regulations is that structures are erected within the building lines of a given property. Should you wish to build on a shared boundary, it may be necessary to obtain written consent from neighbours before the local authorities will consider your application.

Although local regulations may specify the dimensions of foundations, footings and other structural elements, the size of the structure itself (whether a carport or a pergola) is largely personal choice. However, bear in mind that a carport should be large enough to cover your car in order to be useful: guidelines for a structure which will accommodate one car are 3 m x 5.5 m (10 ft x 18 ft), whereas a double carport should be at least 5.5 m x 5.5 m (18 ft x 18 ft). If you own a larger vehicle – a station-wagon, minibus or caravan, for example – take into account its dimensions, opening the doors while you measure the area.

A simple pergola built with precast concrete pillars on the boundary of a property.

The recommended minimum height for a carport is 2.4 m (8 ft) from the finished floor to the underside of the roof covering or crossbeams, though it might be wise to increase this a little if the structure is likely to have to accommodate boats or roof racks.

No structure should be less than 2.1 m (7 ft) high unless it is purely a decorative feature.

You will probably have to submit plans for all structures you plan to build, irrespective of their simplicity. Submissions usually consist of a site plan which indicates boundary lines, existing buildings, trees, swimming pools and so on; elevations and sections of the structure in relation to adjacent levels; and any drainage arrangements. A copy of the building regulations can sometimes be obtained from a local building authority. However, the construction of an open-sided carport or pergola is usually considered to be 'minor building work', and unless you are drawing up your own plans, it is unlikely that you will have to refer to the regulations directly. Your local authority can answer any specific queries you may have, or if you are using the services of a professional person, he or she should be able to provide all the technical data you require (see page 13).

If you intend to convert your carport to a garage with solid brick or block walls at some stage in the future, remember that you will need to build foundations for them beneath the level of the proposed carport floor. For convenience you could include the garage on your plans as a proposed building, and lay additional foundations now, although some local authorities may insist that construction begin within a specific period of time.

Plans will be essential for a pergola of this complexity.

BUILD YOUR OWN CARPORT AND PERGOLA

A modern interpretation of Victorian style enhances a simple timber staircase.

A variety of materials blends well to create a characterful shelter.

walkways and all the other overheads discussed in this book tend to be more functional.

A simple carport or pergola design may be constructed using wooden poles or planed posts spanned by a cut-timber roof structure. Alternatively, uprights may be built from brick, cut or random stone, metal, or even concrete set in fibrecement forms.

Classic pergola designs, especially those created in the Victorian genre, may also be erected using metal hoops. Or you may prefer to utilise old materials if these are available – period cast-iron poles, for instance, are a popular choice.

Whatever materials you choose, any structure may be used as a support for climbing plants. In many cases though, the pergola will become secondary to the plants as they gradually cover the posts and overhead beams. Just be sure that the plants have adequate support and will not cause the timber sections to rot or brickwork to collapse.

COST

This is invariably a consideration – and the first two steps you can take toward effective cost control are thorough planning and careful budgeting. Even if you are going to call in professionals to do the work for you, every effort should be made to avoid expensive mistakes and excessive wastage.

Once you have decided what type of structure you want to build, quantify and cost the project (see pages 40-41). Price everything from cement and stone to bolts and nails. If you are doing it all yourself, consider whether you will need extra labour to help you, and include this cost in your budget. Also estimate a figure for lighting, plants, paint, and any other finishing touches you may want.

If you find that the project is going to be too expensive, you may be able to raise finance through a bank or other financial institution. Alternatively, you can settle for a simpler design, use different materials, or adopt a more flexible building plan which can be completed in phases.

THE ROLE OF THE PROFESSIONAL

As the structures discussed in this book are reasonably substantial, you are likely to need the services of at least one professional who can draw up plans for submission to your local authority. Although there is nothing to stop you from drawing up the plans yourself, official regulations are usually quite specific in their requirements (see page 11), so unless you are familiar with the regulations, this will be money well spent. You can, of course, approach your local authority for information, or employ some other experienced person to help you. At the construction stage, you could hire an artisan to help you, or you could hand over part or all of the project to a contractor.

Architect You may feel that you do not need to spend money on an expert, as this is a simple structure. However, the assistance of a qualified architect can be invaluable at the planning stage, especially if you want to make sure that the design of your new structure blends with the house and that it will be structurally sound. Most architects charge an hourly fee for consultation and will get as involved in the project as you wish. Architectural designers have similar skills.

Draughtsman Architectural firms employ trained draughtsmen to do their working drawings for them, but many of these people prefer to work on a freelance basis instead, preparing drawings for laymen who do not have the necessary skills. If you know what you want, you can safely ask a draughtsman to draw up your plans.

More experienced draughtsmen may be willing to assist with design specifications, and even to oversee the building operation. It is advisable, however, to ask for reliable recommendations from friends or acquaintances.

Landscaper Landscape architects and garden specialists (some of whom have professional qualifications) will often undertake construction work in the garden as part of a general landscaping contract. Before you hire a specialist of this kind, enquire whether he will subcontract the job, or whether he has the resources to do it himself.

Building contractor Most small-scale builders will undertake to do the entire project for you, from submission of plans, through ordering of materials, to building. However, before signing a contract, ask to see examples of other similar structures they have built. You could also discuss the possibility of supplying the materials yourself to cut costs.

Some companies specialise in specific designs such as carports or gazebos. These companies may not be in a position to complete all aspects of the work though, and may prefer other professionals to lay a parking slab or paving, or do the planting, for instance.

Subcontractor A compromise between employing a builder and doing the job yourself is to hire specialist artisans to help you. These people can be either hired by the hour, or paid a fee for the entire job, in which case it is best to negotiate the fee before work begins in order to avoid any costly misunderstandings. You will have to supervise the work yourself, and will therefore need to know something about the building operations in progress.

Specialist consultant Engineers and other specialists may provide a valuable service if the site presents problems. Clay soil, huge rocks and steeply sloping ground can cause complications if proper precautions are not taken at the outset.

An extensive pergola which was professionally designed to modernise the front of an old dwelling. Designer: Erwin Hofmann

This unusual, blue-painted structure helps to draw attention away from the neighbouring house. Designer: Peter Loebenberg

DESIGN AND STYLE

A clean-lined, narrow pergola designed to support plants.

An attractive carport with sturdy, plastered pillars.

The design and style of garden structures is as important as the architecture of your house, and should never be underestimated. Whatever you decide to build, the design of the structure must suit the area in which it is to be located.

While most contemporary structures have a practical function, you should also aim for a pleasing visual effect. A design which has been thought through properly will fit in with the style of both house and garden; those that are ill-conceived or hurriedly built, on the other hand, are likely to look shoddy and out of place.

The visual appeal of carports is frequently overlooked, undoubtedly because of their practical nature. However, a pergola can also look like an afterthought if consideration is not given to all aspects of the outdoor area. Even a pretty gazebo will look odd if the surrounding architectural elements of both house and garden do not complement its design. Care should thus be taken both when choosing the materials for the structure itself and when adding finishing touches such as planting, furniture and lighting.

Garden planning relies to a large extent on common sense, although following a few basic guidelines will help to ensure success.

DESIGN BASICS

A well-designed garden generally has a consistent visual theme, and this should be extended to any structures which are included. If flowerbeds and planting are formal, structures should fit the same mould. An informal plan with curves and island beds calls for a similarly informal approach to building.

Existing architecture influences garden design, so this too must be considered. If you have a quaint Victorian home and are planning to site a carport beside it, building the same kind of no-nonsense, low-maintenance, facebrick structure as your friend recently erected will obviously be quite inappropriate. Similarly, if yours is a clean-lined, modern home, a rustic wooden-pole arrangement will tend to look odd sited alongside it. Instead, opt for pillars that are plastered and painted the same colour as the house, or choose a design that uses cut and planed or laminated timber.

Proportion is always important, in relation to both the size of the property and existing features and buildings. For example, a large structure with heavy overhead beams is likely to look out of place beside an intimate plunge pool or over a small patio. Instead, consider a smaller, arbour-like arrangement which will look more balanced and will not detract from what you already have.

Pergolas and carports may be freestanding, or they may be attached to the house, an outbuilding or a boundary wall. A pergola-covered patio leading from the living rooms of the house will generally create a feeling of space. If you live in a hot

HISTORICAL PERSPECTIVE

Pergolas have been popular for many centuries. We know from murals and archaeological studies at Pompeii that at the time of the Roman empire, they were a standard feature in most aristocratic houses, and were often constructed over courtyards. Arbours, too, date back to ancient civilisations: trellised structures, presumably used for cultivating grape vines, were uncovered in Egypt a century ago. During the Renaissance, Italian garden designers created colonnades and wide loggias sometimes leading to water features, as well as grand pergolas.

The terms 'pergola' and 'arbour' are often used interchangeably, with 'pergola' defined in some dictionaries as an 'arbour or covered walk'. But while 'arbour' implies a shady retreat with some kind of seating, 'pergola' has acquired a much broader meaning, incorporating a wide range of overhead structures which might shelter anything from a formal walkway or entrance to an intimate patio, or which could simply be a feature in the garden.

Traditionally formed with a framework of flexible, green tree stems (which eventually rot), arbours are typically more rustic and informal than pergolas. Sometimes, however, gazebo-like arbours are made of wire or timber latticework. Arbours are usually depicted as being semi-enclosed and covered with plants; some early illustrations indicate that they were roofless, while other ancient arbours reconstructed by archaeologists were open-sided, rectangular structures topped with a canopy, more like the modern pergola in form.

The original gazebo, as its name suggests, was constructed to offer a view of some sort. In recent years, this concept has been lost to some extent, although the designs copied today do tend to fit the traditionally decorative style. Most are square, hexagonal or octagonal in plan, and in contrast to the simple pergola, are frequently constructed with a steeply pitched roof.

One of the most exalted advocates of the pergola was the British architect Sir Edwin Lutyens, who worked hand-in-hand with Gertrude Jekyll, one of the world's greatest professional gardeners. Around the turn of the twentieth century, he designed many outdoor structures which frame views and link buildings architecturally with the outdoors. While most of his layouts are grand and too large for the average suburban plot these days, many of his ideas can be imitated on a smaller scale.

A Victorian-style gazebo.

climate, it will also provide welcome shade to the interior from the summer sun. If not, avoid a heavy roof structure or thick plant cover. Alternatively, you could plant a deciduous creeper which will allow the sunshine in during the cooler months (see page 23).

Regardless of the materials used, carports and pergolas usually consist of uprights teamed with a lighter roof structure, which may be either topped with some form of roofing material (see pages 19-21) or left open.

There are many ways to make your patio a more pleasant place. You could, for example, train fragrant, flowering plants over the pergola, or fill the gaps between the upright posts with latticework or planting to create a feeling of privacy.

A pergola with an ornamental pitched roof may be constructed as a central feature, perhaps where two walkways intersect. Or it could be used as an alternative for an open-sided gazebo, thus adding a period look to the property.

Substantial concrete pillars, positioned on a low wall, support wooden beams.

BUILD YOUR OWN CARPORT AND PERGOLA 15

FLOOR SURFACES

The flooring material chosen for the area beneath any overhead structure must be appropriate for the use to which the structure is to be put. A pretty ground cover will add charm to a small arbour tucked away at the end of a path, but it is obviously impractical for a carport floor. Gravel and asphalt, on the other hand, are acceptable materials for carports, but are not very good options for an outdoor living area.

The way any floor surface is laid will also affect the final appearance of the carport or pergola, as will the texture of the materials used.

Asphalt and tarmac

Ideal for functional carports, these materials are inexpensive and quick to lay. However, asphalt and tarmac are not easy to work with, and must be rolled while hot, so are usually applied by specialist contractors. Cold-mix equivalents are available for the DIY market, but are not as hard-wearing as the real thing. While asphalt and tarmac are not particularly pretty surface materials, the effect can be softened by planting around the edges.

Brick paving

Popular, attractive and durable, brick paving is eminently suitable for both patio and carport floors. It may also be used on driveways, pathways and other adjacent surfaces.

Depending on the effect you want to create and on your budget, either clay or concrete bricks or blocks may be used. Both are available in a variety of colours ranging from burnt orange, red and terracotta, to buff and grey. They may also be laid in a number of ways to create different patterns (see page 44).

Brick paving has the advantage of being able to take huge loads – some paving companies will guarantee their paving to withstand loads of up to 4,000 kg (about 8,800 lb).

Interlocking concrete paving blocks are a practical alternative to brick paving. They are manufactured in various colours, and cost much the same as ordinary concrete pavers. Basically the same techniques used for regular paving are applicable when laying interlocking blocks.

Cobbles

True cobbles are small river stones. They are pressed into mortar which has been laid on a solid concrete base. However, cobbles are not always easy to obtain and they are, in any case, tedious to lay. Furthermore, while the finish is attractive, stones tend to make a very irregular surface which is uncomfortable to walk on. Nowadays, several companies manufacture regular 'cobbles' from concrete or reconstituted stone. These are more like old-fashioned granite setts and are suitable for both patio and carport floors.

Concrete

A single concrete slab is a cheap and common parking surface which is easily laid by the amateur builder (see pages 42-43). Although there is no reason why a single concrete slab should not be used beneath a pergola, individual precast slabs are more attractive since they may be laid with grass or a pretty ground cover between them. Alternatively, consider combining the concrete with other materials such as timber or brick.

Gravel

Although natural river stones are used in some places (pea gravel, for instance, is common in Britain), gravel is often made from crushed stone. While this makes an inexpensive and acceptable parking surface, it should be thoroughly compacted to give your car tyres a good grip. Ask for crushed stone suitable for a base course, and not the 'single-sized' stone used for concrete mixes, as this may cause car tyres to slip. Gravel areas must always have some kind of edging to prevent the stones from spreading onto adjacent grass or flowerbeds.

Brick paving is perfect for a carport.

Natural tiles in a striking combination with concrete cast in situ.

Laterite, a fine gravel and clay mixture which is sprayed with water and rolled to a smooth surface, may also be used for carport and patio floors, although it is more commonly used for walkways.

Grass
Most people prefer a hard floor surface beneath structures, and in areas with either a high rainfall or very little rain, this is probably best. If you live in a climate with moderate rainfall, though, you could plant grass instead, as it is unlikely to get waterlogged or turn brown. In fact, if you cannot afford the floor surface of your choice, grass can be a good interim option.

Ground cover
A number of ground-cover species can be grown beneath purely ornamental structures as they do not experience much foot traffic. Some will create a carpet of colour, others a blanket of green foliage. Various species of creeping herb will introduce a pleasant fragrance underfoot.

Pebble paving
River stones or pebbles can be bonded together in a special mixture of resin and concrete, and then applied over concrete to form a continuous surface about 13 mm (½ in) thick. Pebble paving is attractive and practical, but is not available as a DIY material. It is also fairly pricey and available through only a few companies.

Slate
This natural material, which is laid on a concrete base, is available in both regular and irregular shapes (laid as crazy paving) and as cut tiles. It is suitable for patios, driveways and carport floors.

Stone
Cut stone slabs make a lovely natural floor surface anywhere in the garden. Unfortunately though, the lack of experienced artisans to cut the stone makes this material expensive and hard to obtain, and this severely limits its use.

Grass is an inexpensive option worth considering.

Crazy paving laid on an informal patio.

Slate tiles are laid on concrete as the floor of a carport.

Railway sleepers suit the style of this rustic barbecue area.

Nowadays, reconstituted stone, which is moulded in factories to produce regular shapes, is widely available. It is laid on a bed of sand in exactly the same way as clay or concrete pavers.

Tiles

Although suitable for patio surfaces, ceramic tiles are not generally recommended for carports as they crack relatively easily. There is no reason, however, why most terrazzo, terracotta or other natural clay tiles should not be laid as carport flooring, provided that there is a solid concrete base. If you are in any doubt, contact the manufacturer before purchasing the materials.

Timber

Commonly used as a decking material, timber is suitable for use in most parts of the garden, and is often found as a flooring material for outdoor structures of all kinds. Availability of different kinds of wood varies from place to place. Some of the most popular varieties include afrormosia, an attractive, yellow-brown hardwood from West Africa; balau, which is strong and durable, and well-suited to hot, humid climates; beech, a pale, straight-grained wood; Californian redwood, a fairly hard softwood which resists decay; meranti, a versatile Malaysian timber which has become scarce in recent years; and teak, an expensive, top-quality hardwood. Enquire at your local supplier which kind of timber would best suit local weather conditions and the type of structure you intend to build.

Where they are available, old railway sleepers, which are made from extremely hard woods, are a popular choice. Sliced tree trunks are also an option, although they do not always wear very well. Both have a tendency to become somewhat slippery in wet weather. To ensure a good, firm grip underfoot, sleepers should ideally be separated by planting, although this is best avoided when sliced tree trunks are used as it is difficult to trim.

OVERHEAD SHELTER

Protection from the elements will be a major factor in determining the type of roof covering, if any, chosen for your pergola, overhead or carport. Cost will obviously also be a factor, but if you do not have sufficient funds, it is never cost-effective to settle for poor quality materials as they may need replacing within a short period of time.

As with all other materials used for the structure, the type of roofing chosen must complement the materials used for the house and elsewhere in the garden. If your carport is to be an extension of the house, you may be able to use the same type of roof covering for the new structure. If not, pay careful attention to details like fascias, piers and pillars, matching the style, and if possible, building materials and finishes, including plaster and paint colours.

When working with opaque sheeting, it is helpful to stretch a string across the roof from one end of each beam to the other so that you do not lose track of the position of the beam as you nail down the sheeting.

Aluminium

Although considerably more expensive than corrugated iron roof sheeting, this metal is popular in coastal areas where rust is a problem. However, while lightweight and easy to work with, aluminium is generally handled by professionals as it is easily damaged and as special equipment is needed to cut it. It is commonly available in interlocking sheets of up to 3 m x 6 m (10 ft x 20 ft), and some suppliers will cut it to size for you.

Aluminium awnings can sometimes be bought from specialist companies.

Bituminous felt

This black, waterproof covering is an inexpensive material which will give protection from both sun and rain. Available in rolls of varying widths, it can be nailed to any wooden structure, and joints and nail holes sealed with bitumen paste. It is more commonly used as a roofing material for carports than for other garden structures. Once

A retractable canvas awning shades a pretty, seaside pergola.

it has weathered, bituminous felt can be resealed by painting with bitumen to make it last longer. There are several bituminous waterproofing compounds available for this purpose.

Canvas

Fixed and retractable canvas awnings are common over patios. They are available in a wide range of colours, designed to complement all outdoor décor. The fabric, which is usually treated to make it water-resistant, is strong, although its lifespan can be somewhat limited.

Corrugated iron

A reasonably inexpensive material, corrugated iron is a particularly popular choice for carports built in areas where rain is not a major weathering factor. Like fibreglass and fibrecement, it is available in various profiles, of which S-rib and inverted box rib (IBR) are the most common. Corrugated iron can be bought galvanised or colour-coated. It is attached to the roof beams with special screws which are either hammered or turned in.

Fibrecement

Probably the heaviest roof sheeting available, fibrecement is often also the cheapest option. It comes in a selection of profiles suitable for providing shelter over a wide range of structures: 'Big Six' and 'Canadian' configurations assist drainage and are therefore among the designs most frequently used for carports. Because of its weight, fibrecement requires sturdy roof trusses, but is less likely than other materials to blow away in very windy conditions.

Some fibrecement products still contain a small amount of asbestos (which can be harmful to one's health if inhaled), so it is important that you adhere to the manufacturer's safety recommendations when cutting or drilling this material.

Fibreglass

A popular material for covering both pergolas and carports, fibreglass is available in a number of standard widths and profiles, including corrugated S-rib and IBR. It also comes in a variety of colours, the most popular of which are probably transparent, green and white.

Fibreglass is lightweight, easy to handle and therefore ideal for the home handyman. It should be drilled before being secured to the crossbeams with roofing screws.

Plants

Creepers and climbers will improve the appearance of almost any garden structure. Most will also provide shade in hot weather and some protection from the sun's harmful rays. A pergola is a typical and effective support for climbing plants which, if properly trained, will eventually form a beautiful living ceiling over the structure. There are many suitable plants you can use, including honeysuckle, clematis and beautifully scented jasmine, as well as various vines and rambling roses, which will add fragrance and a special ambience to the area (see page 23). However, it is important to consider the specific site, soil and climatic conditions, all of which will have a direct effect on what you plant and how well your plants will grow. If you are not sure what to plant, though, check with your local nursery.

Polycarbonate

This smooth, modern material, which looks like glass or perspex, is eminently suitable for all structures, especially carports which have been designed to protect motor vehicles. It is, however, more expensive than other roofing materials. Manufactured in the form of sheeting from a strong plastic-type material, experts say it will not crack or fade. It usually comes in transparent, bronze and opaque white sheets, which may be flat or corrugated, and which are generally available in the same standard widths as fibreglass and metal sheeting.

This green-striped shadecloth cover provides shelter from the sun.

Reeds

Both Spanish reeds and bamboo are attractive and effective natural materials to use for patio and carport roofing. Although reeds and bamboo are not always available commercially, they are a good choice if there is a natural supply in your area.

Gathered from river beds, reeds must be stripped of their tough outer layer and cut to size before they can be used. If they are to provide reasonable protection from sun and rain, reeds should be set close together with thick and thin ends alternating. They should also be used while they are still green and pliable so that they dry out in position, otherwise they are likely to bend and crack, making them less effective and harder to work with. To prevent the reeds from splitting, drill small holes where the nails are to be hammered in before fastening them to the beams. Alternatively, they can be tied to the structure.

Reeds create a rustic mood.

20 BUILD YOUR OWN CARPORT AND PERGOLA

Shadecloth

A popular material in areas with hot summers, shadecloth is perfect for providing shelter from the sun, and is available in various densities offering 30% to 85% protection. Although it will not protect you or your car from rain or even heavy dew, shadecloth will act as an umbrella in the event of hail.

Shadecloth comes in a number of plain colours, including horticultural green, black and blue, and in a range of brightly coloured stripes. It can be bought at hardware shops and superstores in 3 m (10 ft) widths.

This material should be cut with a soldering iron to prevent fraying, and can be nailed or stapled to the wood or attached with special toothed connectors. It cannot be glued, and will deteriorate if attached to wood treated with creosote. When covering larger structures, a special monofilament may be used to stitch pieces of shadecloth together.

Tarpaulin

Waterproof tarpaulin will shield the structure from direct sun and give protection from the rain. It may be used as an awning in place of canvas, or tied on when required by securing it through reinforced 'eyes'. Various tarpaulin grades are available, some of which are manufactured from PVC (polyvinyl chloride – a type of plastic) and reinforced with polyester. Since it is manufactured primarily for the trucking industry, it is reasonably durable but not always very attractive.

Thatch

Although this material is expensive in some countries, and requires a skilled craftsman, it is particularly suitable for pergolas built with wooden poles. The recommended minimum pitch for a thatched roof is 45°, although flatter thatch coverings are possible.

Tiles

If the roof of your house is tiled, you may want to use matching tiles for the roof of your carport, or even for an entertaining patio. Any type may be used (although cost may be an inhibiting factor), and the material chosen will affect the pitch of the roof. Some smooth tiles, including slate, may be laid with a minimum 15° pitch, while others with a rough, granular finish should have at least a 26° pitch.

Period-style gazebos (see page 15) usually have quite steeply pitched roofs which are frequently tiled or slated.

Timber

A lath ceiling, consisting of thin strips of sawn or split timber similar to those commonly used for latticework, will give you an attractive shelter. They may also be used to create a grid pattern. A simple, pre-made trellis, available from some garden centres or timber yards, is another option.

Closely spaced laths filter the sunlight.

A tiled roof over a small pergola made with poles.

BUILD YOUR OWN CARPORT AND PERGOLA 21

A simple trellis screen supports plants on a roof garden.

Latticework creates an effective but unobtrusive screen.

SCREENING

While overhead shelter is often considered to be one of the most significant elements of any pergola or carport design, additional screening around the sides will augment its usefulness. The location of the structure, the degree of protection or privacy you require, and the ambience you wish to create will determine the type of screen you erect.

There is a vast choice of materials which you can use for screening. However, make sure that the material you choose matches or blends in with those used for the structure itself.

Fencing

Fences are commonly used to enclose gardens, but not all types are suitable for screening carports or pergolas. Low timber fencing is probably the most appropriate, but metal or wire fencing can be effective for screening if used in conjunction with plants. Any reasonably solid fence, however, will make a good windbreak and block out noise.

Latticework

Trellises and lattice panels are made of thin strips of wood crossed either horizontally and vertically or diagonally. Trellises are usually erected to support climbing plants, and can be either freestanding or attached to a wall, while latticework is often used as a decorative feature on its own, as part of a structure, or combined with planting. Either may be used as an attractive alternative to more conventional fencing, and without blocking out too much light, will screen the area both visually and from the wind.

If latticework or planting extends the full height of the structure, the feeling of intimacy and seclusion may be increased. On the other hand, by erecting it only to waist height, you will have the advantage of a wider view of the garden, effectively enlarging the visual proportions of the area.

Planting

Often the simplest screen is one which is planted. The most substantial kind is a hedge, although it obviously takes time to create, and should be well trimmed and shaped if it is to lend form to the area. However, the style of your garden must also be taken into account; an informal layout, with irregularly shaped flowerbeds and a rustic structure may demand a different approach.

A simple way of screening with plants alone is to grow climbers up wire or some other support system strung out between the posts. Alternatively, plant a mixture of colourful shrubs in between the structural elements to create an informal hedge. Fill in any gaps in this 'hedge' you have created with annuals until substantial growth has been established.

Walls

Although a solid wall is often included as part of the structure of a pergola or carport (for instance, when it is attached to one of the walls of the house), it is not necessarily a good idea for screening purposes. If a small area is completely enclosed by walls, it could become unpleasantly windy in bad weather. Instead, opt for a reasonably low wall which extends across a short distance, or consider building a wall with staggered bricks or using decorative breeze blocks or perforated bricks.

The advantage of solid brick or concrete block walls is that planters, niches and other decorative features may more easily be built in to add interest and appeal. Ultimately, the choice you make depends on the site and on your personal taste.

CHOOSING CLIMBERS AND CREEPERS

While perennials, shrubs and flowering annuals planted around a pergola and carport will add form, colour and texture to the overall impression created, climbers and creepers will enhance the appearance of the structure itself.

The function and design of the structure, as well as its location and the materials used, will all play a vital role in your choice of plants. While rambling and climbing roses are a traditional choice for pergolas, they are generally not a good idea for carports, which are busy, functional areas. They may look pretty, but prickly thorns will frustrate anyone trying to offload shopping and other goods! Grapevines (*Vitis* spp) are another popular choice, especially over patios. Although decorative and attractive, however, some varieties are notoriously messy during the fruit season and are best avoided as a cover over carports.

Deciduous plants If a carport or pergola is adjacent to the house and likely to cast an unwanted shadow in winter, deciduous plants are often the best bet. Clematis is a universal favourite; well-suited to colder climes, it is also a good choice for a busy walkway or small arbour which will benefit from sunshine in winter. Wisteria (in particular *Wisteria sinensis*, which bears long, beautiful clusters of white or mauve flowers) is another popular species.

Although some of the *Lonicera* species are evergreen and hardy in sunny conditions, English honeysuckle (*L. periclymenum*) is a suitable deciduous variety, and one which will reward you with vigorous growth. In warm, frost-free areas, the light but hardy Chilean jasmine (*Mandevilla laxa*) is another possibility.

Evergreens The colourful Mexican blood trumpet (*Distictis buccinatoria*) is an obvious option for pergolas. It is vigorous and reasonably quick-growing, and will withstand some frost. Others include the robust climber, Carolina jasmine (*Gelsemium sempervirens*), which bears clusters of scented blooms; the fragrant star jasmine (*Trachelospermum jasminoides*) and ever-popular common white jasmine (*Jasmine officinale*); as well as golden shower (*Pyrostegia venusta*) with its particularly long-lasting and magnificent show of bright orange flowers. A semi-hardy climber, it must be protected from cold winds.

If you live in a warm, frost-free area, other possibilities are the mauve bignonia (*Clytostoma callistegioides*), the golden trumpet vine (*Allamanda cathartica*) which bears yellow trumpet-shaped flowers, and several of the fascinating *Passiflora* species, better known as the passion flower.

Hot climate plants In temperate and subtropical areas, the orange black-eyed Susan (*Thunbergia alata*), and *T. grandiflora* with its large, mauve flowers, may be grown over carports and patio pergolas. The many subspecies of bougainvillea are all certain favourites which will add welcome splashes of colour. Once well-established, bougainvillea is a heavy plant so it should be restricted to solid structures. The vigorous Zimbabwe climber (*Podranea brycei*), which bears masses of pretty, pink trumpet-shaped flowers, is another possibility, as is the attractive coral creeper (*Antigonon leptopus*), which bears vivid pink flowers in summer and autumn. You may also like to try growing the spectacular jade vine (*Strongylodon macrobotrys*). This plant has magnificent, long racemes bearing unusual blue-green flowers; to see jade vine at its best, train it over a high structure.

Frost-resistant plants There are several attractive species of jasmine, including the star jasmine, which are well suited to colder climates. Although semi-deciduous in cooler regions, the sweet-smelling Chinese jasmine (*Jasminum polyanthum*) is a light, reasonably quick-growing evergreen creeper. Another is the Australian bower of beauty (*Pandorea jasminoides*) which, because it is not a particularly vigorous grower, can be successfully grown with other creepers. Other popular climbers which will resist frost include wisteria, clematis, honeysuckle (the *Lonicera* species) and most climbing roses. Most of these plants will struggle to grow in dry or humid conditions.

A well-established vine on a pergola shades a patio crammed with pot plants.

Wisteria provides shade in summer and fills the air with its perfume when it flowers in spring.

DRAINAGE

If you are building away from the house on stable, level ground, and you do not intend to construct a solid roof, drainage will not be an issue. Nevertheless, the matter of drainage should never be overlooked. If rainwater is allowed to accumulate, you could find yourself with an unusable quagmire in wet weather.

Floor surface

When working alongside an existing building, it is essential for the finished surface to be at least 150 mm (6 in) below the floor slab's damp-proof course (DPC). Made of thick polythene sheeting, the DPC is the principle means of minimising damp in buildings. It is laid under concrete floor slabs and at the base of external walls. Although not always visible after construction, the position of the DPC is usually relatively easy to determine.

In addition, water must always be channelled away from the building. The simplest way of doing this is to slope the finished floor surface away from the house (see pages 28-29). You may also need to run a channel from the floor of the structure to an existing gully or drain, or to create a small soakaway filled with broken bricks and stones.

On sites where clay is a problem, it is also sensible to compact hardcore or crushed stone beneath foundations and footings, and even under paving and concrete slabs.

Plastic sheeting is frequently laid under brick paving, although this is often done to check unsightly weed growth rather than to prevent moisture from rising. It may also be laid under concrete, especially when a patio or carport is built alongside the house, or if you are planning to tile the surface and want to ensure a dry base. A fairly thin 250 micron plastic is quite adequate.

If you have a steep plot, you will probably have to terrace part of it in order to build any type of structure. It may also be necessary to include a retaining wall in the design.

The space behind a retaining wall should be filled with compacted hardcore for drainage. In addition, weepholes must be left at the base of the wall: either insert piping through the width of the wall, or leave quarter-brick gaps, approximately a metre (3 ft) apart, in the second course of bricks in the wall.

If you plan to build a retaining wall higher than about a metre (3 ft), it will be wise to enlist the help of a professional such as an engineer.

Roof covering

Most pergola and carport roofs are fairly flat, sometimes deceptively so, but there must always be a slight slope for drainage. Usually this slope is not more than 3° to 5° (1 in 20 to 1 in 10 gradient), and in most cases, it pitches away from the building if the structure is not freestanding. The slope should in any case carry water in the direction of a channel, soakaway or drain.

Guttering is attached to the fascia with brackets.

Guttering

Whenever a solid roof structure is chosen for a pergola or carport design, guttering and downpipes must be included. If the water is not channelled away from timber roof beams, they will eventually rot.

The most common materials used for guttering are PVC, fibrecement, and galvanised metal. Ideally choose something that matches, or at least complements, the guttering used on your house and outbuildings.

Fascia boards usually abut guttering along the front of any roof. While the most common material is wood, aluminium and fibrecement fascias are also available.

Flashings

A variety of standard flashings (usually made from aluminium or galvanised steel) are available to prevent water from seeping from the roof structure into or down any adjoining walls. Side-wall and head-wall flashings are used to cover the area where the roof meets a vertical wall, and cover flashing is built into the wall, over the edge of the side- or head-wall flashing, to allow for the expansion and contraction of the roof in changing weather conditions.

A well-sealed drainage channel where sloping roofs meet.

24 BUILD YOUR OWN CARPORT AND PERGOLA

SECURITY

Although it is not always a central issue when planning garden structures, security can be of primary importance when a carport is sited on or near the boundary of any property.

If the carport is to be situated within a walled or fenced area, away from the road, there may already be gates securing it. Where there is direct access to the street, the most obvious solution is to install gates across the front of the carport. Remote-controlled gates are the best choice, as they save you from having to climb in and out of the car every time you leave or return home, and thus make you less vulnerable; however, they are also the most expensive option. Another more elaborate possibility is to build in garage doors, or even automatic doors, on the boundary. This will, in a way, give you the best of both worlds – security without the expense and encumbrance of an actual building.

A very cheap and simple, but fairly effective, way of securing a carport without a gate is to fix a chain from pillar to pillar. Alternatively, a plain wooden boom can be fixed across the front. Metal fold-down barriers which are bolted to the surface are also available. Bear in mind that while these procedures will protect your vehicle from being stolen, they will still allow a thief access to the car and will therefore not safeguard radios or other items which may have been left inside.

If your house already has external lighting, examine its effectiveness in terms of security. If it is not adequate, you may consider installing security switches, which turn lights on and off automatically, and which are useful both inside and outside the house. There are various sorts available, all of which will suggest to potential burglars that there is someone at home at all times. Fixed timing switches, which are controlled by a programmable unit, are particularly useful for patios, pathways and so on. Light-sensing devices, on the other hand, are a better option for carports and entrances.

Automatic garage doors secure a carport from the road.

These are activated by natural light, and will automatically come on at dusk and turn off at dawn. Although the better units are connected to electrical circuit boards, cheaper external light fittings which are triggered in the same way are also available. Many security systems also incorporate lighting which is activated automatically by movement, using passive infrared sensors. The lights and sensors can sometimes be bought from a DIY store and fitted yourself.

Remote-controlled gates prevent intruders from gaining access to the two carports depicted above.

BUILD YOUR OWN CARPORT AND PERGOLA

It is important to illuminate a carport.

LIGHTING

Exterior lighting is essential, not only for security (see page 25) and general safety, but also for extending the usefulness of your garden. Any outdoor area which is not illuminated at night will be a potential hazard in the dark. Furthermore, if you are going to go to the trouble of building a pergola and creating an attractive patio area, it makes sense to incorporate proper lighting so that you can entertain outside and enjoy the fruits of your labour at night as well as during the day.

Consider whether existing lighting illuminates the site of the planned structure adequately. If you are building a carport, will the lighting provided enable you to get from your car to the house without tripping over obstacles in the dark?

If there is no suitable lighting on your property, consider all the options. Spotlights, which cast a direct shaft of light in one direction, are highly practical, especially at points of entry and where security is a factor. These may be mounted on the wall of your house, on one of the upright posts of a pergola, or within a carport. Of course, lighting is also decorative; a few simple garden spots used to emphasise features will immediately enliven the area.

Floodlights are seldom used to illuminate a patio alone as the broad, intense beam can be overwhelming, but they are useful for very large properties. If the pergola has been built alongside a swimming pool or tennis court, they could be a practical choice. Floodlights are also good for security purposes.

When lighting a patio, aim for a good general light. The best way of achieving this is with wall-mounted fittings, bollards and freestanding garden lamps. Coloured lights can be decorative, but consider the effect different hues will have. The best choice for the garden is generally green or amber; blue is cold while red gives plants an unnatural look.

Remember that any fittings which you choose should be manufactured specially for outdoor use. A unit which is not sealed for protection from rain is not suitable as it can be dangerous. Waterproof or armour cabling must always be used, and this should be buried underground wherever possible. Note where any cables are located to avoid accidental damage when digging in the garden. Wiring should also be connected to the mains supply by an authorised person.

If your pergola is built alongside the house, you will probably be able to utilise the internal electrical arrangement. If it is some distance from the house, you may require a separate circuit; this could, however, be linked to an existing outdoor electrical circuit (installed for a swimming pool or hot tub, garage or other outbuilding). Although there is nothing to stop you from laying cables and fixing fittings yourself, electricity is potentially lethal, and it makes good sense that all basic electrical work be undertaken, or at least supervised, by a registered electrician.

FINISHING TOUCHES

There are many ways of adding that final touch to even the plainest, most functional structure: tubs of flowering shrubs placed around the perimeter of a carport; pot plants in pretty baskets suspended from a pergola; a spurting fountain at the end of a covered walkway; statues or urns at ground level or set in niches in a wall; even simply a coordinated colour scheme.

The secret, though, is to choose decorative elements which will look natural and appropriate rather than jumbled or cluttered. The guidelines you need can all be taken from good garden design.

Good lighting is essential if you want to use your patio at night.

Containers

There is a huge range of containers for outdoor use, made of materials such as terracotta, fibrecement, wood and ceramic. Set on plinths and pedestals or on the ground, and planted with pretty annuals or colourful flowering shrubs, they will all add appeal to any garden structure.

Containers often look most effective when grouped, but take care not to create unnecessary obstacles for people using the patio or carport.

Furniture

Outdoor furniture, for everyday use and entertaining alike, can be both practical and attractive, and chosen carefully, it will always make a patio a more useful and pleasant place. It may be either built-in or freestanding, depending on the design and style of the pergola and surrounding area.

If your structure has brick pillars, or if you have included a barbecue in the design, simple benches with wooden seats supported by low piers are easily incorporated. If the overhead is constructed on a timber deck, the same material may also be used for tables and benches, as well as for storage boxes which can double as extra seating.

There is a wide range of materials and styles available when it comes to choosing freestanding garden furniture. Ordinary precast concrete is a common choice. Left unpainted, it will probably become slightly worn and mossy with time, blending in beautifully with the plant life. Elegant metal furniture and benches made of a combination of metal and wood are also favoured; it is important to ensure that both materials are properly treated to withstand the weather. Plastic furniture is generally comfortable and hard-wearing, and brightened up with cushions, it will enhance the area.

Traditional deck chairs are another possibility, and have the advantage of being easy to store. Cane and wicker furniture is often used outdoors, but it is only really suitable for use on patios where a solid roof structure will prevent it from weathering badly.

Cane furniture and an abundance of pot plants enhance a patio.

Bright yellow cushions add colour to a patio used for entertaining.

Hanging baskets

Plants suspended from the overhead beams of pergolas and carports can look charming if well cared for and regularly watered. Take care not to hang the baskets in a position where those using the area will bump into them. If the structure is in a windy spot, pots and tubs will be a more sensible option.

Ornaments

Garden ornaments should fit the size and scale of the area you are decorating. Care must also be taken to place them appropriately. Wall-mounted plaques and panels, fountains and plant containers are suitable for any pergola or carport which is attached to a wall. Statues and sculptures may often be set in the corner of a patio, or in a niche built into a wall. If your pergola covers a walkway in the garden, a statue may look more effective as the focal point at one end. You may prefer to place a sundial here, although strictly speaking, this traditional instrument should not be set under cover, even if you never use it to tell the time.

CONSTRUCTION PRINCIPLES

The design and style you choose for any garden structure will determine the materials required, but before you start, ensure that you can master the relevant techniques and confidently handle all the tools needed to work with the chosen materials.

The basic construction principles and methods used to erect a simple carport or pergola are certainly within the capabilities of most handymen. The secret is to familiarise yourself with the rudiments and stick to them while you work.

THE BASICS
Common sense will tell you that all components need to be vertical and level. Supporting poles must not tilt; bricks and blocks must be laid level and square; paving must be flat and even. You may be working with the best quality materials, but if you do not ensure that your workmanship is square, level and plumb, you will not achieve the professional kind of finish that we all appreciate.

Square
If the corners of a structure are at right angles, it will be square. Of course, this principle will not be relevant if the pergola design is acutely angled or circular, or has any curved sides, but it is often applicable when building with bricks or blocks.

When setting out a design with right-angled corners, it is simple to check that it is square by using the 3:4:5 method (see page 31). When you build up the brickwork you will need to use a builder's square, which will enable you to check constantly that the rising corners are at 90°.

Level
In brickwork, all horizontal surfaces must be absolutely level. You can ensure this by checking foundations and footings, as well as each brick course you lay, with a spirit level. If the bubble in the horizontal vial is centred, the surface is level. When using this useful tool on large surfaces (when paving or throwing a concrete slab, for instance) it is common practice to set the spirit level on a long straight-edged piece of wood.

A line level may be used to ensure that brick pillars are progressing evenly,

A carport erected in front of a garage. Beams and crosspieces are square and level.

28 BUILD YOUR OWN CARPORT AND PERGOLA

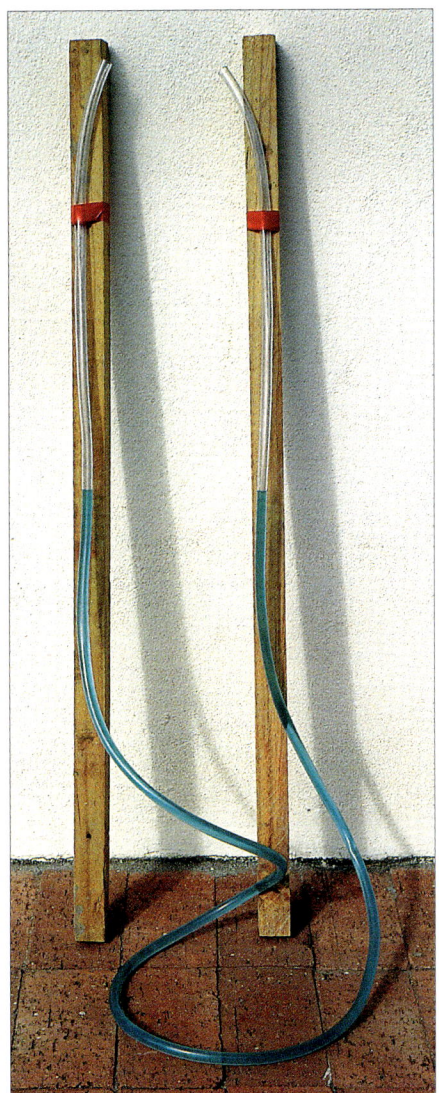

A simple water level is an invaluable aid when tackling any building project.

or to check that a builder's line is correctly positioned.

Paved areas should slope slightly for drainage, and you will have to take this into account. When paving, it is therefore helpful to set up a line corresponding with the slope of the finished surface. Do not rely on guesswork; instead, use a spacer block under your spirit level or straightedge to keep the angle consistent, and then set up the line. To achieve a gradient of 1 in 40, use a 25 mm (1 in) block of wood for each metre (3 ft 3 in).

You can also use a water level to set up a drainage slope, or, for that matter, to ensure that your building site is level. This method is particularly useful over a long stretch or when you need to ensure consistency around a corner. All you need is some transparent tubing, long enough for the requirements of your project, or an ordinary hosepipe with small pieces of transparent tubing fitted in each end. Fill the tube or hosepipe with water and attach it to two pegs set in the ground at any given height. Since water finds its own level, you will immediately see whether to remove more earth or to fill in.

A water level is also invaluable when building a structure with timber uprights. Once you have concreted the posts into the ground, use it to check that the tops are exactly level with one another. If not, simply saw off enough wood to make them the same height.

Plumb
Vertical surfaces of all walls and timber posts must also be aligned and level. A spirit level with both a vertical and a horizontal vial is most commonly used to check for plumb. Alternatively, you can use a plumb bob, which is especially useful for ensuring that the corners of brick or block pillars are straight and upright.

FOUNDATIONS
If you are building with bricks and mortar, timber or metal, all upright pillars and poles must be securely anchored or constructed on a sound footing. You will also need to dig strip foundations for any walls or screens included in your pergola or carport design, and you may have to throw a concrete slab prior to paving if the ground is unstable.

Minimum dimensions for foundations and footings are specified by building regulations (see page 11), although some local authorities may enforce more stringent specifications.

Concrete
A basic concrete mix consists of cement, sand, stone and water, often combined with plasticiser to make it more pliable. Use ordinary Portland cement, widely available in sealed 50 kg (112 lb) bags; clean building sand (called sharp sand in some countries), sold in bags of about 50 kg (112 lb), or supplied in bulk by the cubic metre or cubic foot; 19 mm (¾ in) or 13.2 mm (½ in) crushed stone; and potable tap water.

Dry premixed materials are also available. These are very useful for small projects, including footings for garden structures. Purchasing concrete this way, however, is more expensive than buying the constituent materials individually.

The quantities and proportions you use will depend on the work to be done. However, low-strength concrete is quite adequate for the foundation of most simple structures. If you are working with 19 mm (¾ in) stone, the recommended proportions of cement, sand and stone for hand compaction are 1:4:4, measured by volume. If you opt for a smaller 13.2 mm (½ in) stone, which is certainly easier to mix by hand, less stone should be used – alter the proportions to 1:4:3. If a stronger mix is required, a suitable ratio for the larger stone is 1:3:3, and for the smaller stone, 1:3:2. If necessary, an engineer will advise.

There is no need to measure the water to be used. Simply mix the cement and sand together until the colour is uniform; form a hollow in the middle and add a small amount of liquid at a time, shovelling from the outsides to the centre until you have a workable consistency. Add the stone last, with a little more water if the concrete is too dry.

When using a concrete mixer, load the stone first, together with some water. This prevents cement from building up around the blades of the machine. Add the cement next, and then the sand and enough water to achieve a soft, porridgey consistency.

If you are sinking metal or timber posts into the ground, these must be supported with some form of bracing to ensure that they are absolutely vertical and do not fall over. Once you have checked for plumb with a spirit level, shovel the concrete into the hole and tamp down well with the back of your shovel to compact it and expel all air bubbles.

A spirit level is used to ensure that poles are plumb.

A screen wall and pillar are constructed on a strip foundation.

Foundations for brickwork must be allowed to set before building commences. The concrete must be kept moist while it is curing – hose it lightly with water or cover it with hessian or plastic. Avoid exposure to drying winds, hot sunshine and frost. Ideally, it should be left to cure for five to seven days, although in practice building often begins a day or two after throwing the foundations.

Dimensions

The dimensions of foundations and footings will depend on your particular design, as well as on soil conditions in your garden. Nevertheless, they should always be at least 200 mm (8 in) deep, and more substantial if a heavy roof is to be incorporated. A useful rule of thumb when estimating the width of any foundation for brickwork or blockwork is that it should equal the thickness of the wall or pillar plus twice the depth of the concrete. Thus a 200 mm (8 in) deep footing for a 400 mm x 400 mm (1 ft 4 in x 1 ft 4 in) pillar should be at least 800 mm (2 ft 8 in) wide. If you are in any doubt, increase the size of the footing or seek professional advice.

While some people bed wooden poles directly in the ground, compacting around the poles to stabilise them, it is best to set them in concrete. In fact, a concrete foundation is essential if the structure has a solid roof, as uplift (which occurs when wind gusts under the roof) could result in it collapsing if it is not securely anchored.

Metal poles should always be bedded in reasonably substantial footings at least 600 mm (2 ft) deep, while the base of precast concrete pillars should also be set in a concrete foundation.

When digging foundations for poles, it may be tempting to use a mechanical auger. However, this tool will excavate a hole which is smaller than the size recommended for foundations, and this in turn will affect the strength of the foundations. If you do use one, you will have to bore much deeper into the ground to prevent the pole from coming loose.

Above-ground anchorage

When working with wood, the most common alternative to setting the base in a concrete footing is to use metal base plates. Many people prefer above-ground anchorage as it reduces the likelihood of wood rot. Various anchor plates for posts are available off the shelf for cut timber, but you will probably have to get an engineering firm to make something to secure wooden poles, for instance sturdy galvanised iron bent in an L-shape.

Whatever form of anchorage you use, it will be necessary to throw a foundation or slab upon which it can be fixed, unless there is already a solid base. Although a concrete slab might be thinner, an acceptable minimum depth for individual footings is 200 mm (8 in). As an alternative to a conventional footing, you may prefer to use a tube form which will give you a neat finish, even if the concrete shows above ground. These are made of cardboard and are available in several sizes. If the footing extends above ground level, any visible tubing is removed once the concrete has set.

A post anchor bolted in place.

30 BUILD YOUR OWN CARPORT AND PERGOLA

SETTING OUT

The first step in any building project is to set out the site according to the dimensions and layout of your plan.

Square and rectangular structures
Unless your carport or pergola structure is to be circular or have acute or obtuse angles, you will have to ensure that each corner is exactly square. The simplest way of doing this is to use the 3:4:5 method, as shown below.

Setting out a carport measuring 4 m x 3.5 m (13 ft x 11 ft 6 in) from outer corner to outer corner of the pillars is a relatively easy matter. The dimensions of the footings will depend on the structure itself; in this case the pillars, to be built from concrete blocks, will measure 400 mm x 400 mm (1 ft 4 in x 1 ft 4 in). To support these, foundation footings should measure 800 mm x 800 mm (2 ft 8 in x 2 ft 8 in) across, and about 300 mm (1 ft) deep. If you draw the dimensions to a smaller scale on paper first, you will see that the distances between the inner sides of the pillars will be 3.2 m (10 ft 6 in) and 2.7 m (8 ft 10 in). 200 mm (8 in) of each footing will therefore extend beyond the framework at each corner.

Having decided on the location of the carport, knock a peg into the ground at one corner. Using a steel square or a wooden square (see page 38), measure 3.5 m (11 ft 6 in) in one direction and 4 m (13 ft) at right angles to this line. Insert a peg in the ground at each of these points. To check the angle using the 3:4:5 method, knock another peg into the ground 3 m (10 ft) from the corner on the shorter side, and then measure the distance between this peg and the one already inserted 4 m (13 ft) from the corner. It should be exactly 5 m (16 ft 4 in) away. If not, adjust the angle slightly until the measurement, and therefore the angle, is correct.

Now measure the other two sides and knock a peg into the ground where they meet. Check all the corners to ensure that each one is at 90°. To double-check them, measure the diagonals; they should be the same length and, in this case, should measure just over 5.3 m (17 ft 4 in). To work out the distance mathematically, determine the square root of (side A^2 + side B^2), that is, $\sqrt{(3.5 \text{ m})^2 + (4 \text{ m})^2}$ = 5.315 m ($\sqrt{(11 \text{ ft } 6 \text{ in})^2 + (13 \text{ ft})^2}$ = 17.357 ft, or 17 ft 4¼ in).

The next step is to mark the position of all four footings. You can use lime, white cement, chalk or even flour to do this. The easiest way is to take your pegs and set up a builder's line along the perimeter of the building site, extending beyond the corners by 200 mm (8 in). Then, using the line as a guide, mark the ground 600 mm (2 ft) from each peg, in both directions. Using a builder's square for accuracy, join up the four points to form a square.

Circular designs
If your pergola is to be circular, the best way to set out the site is to use a home-made compass. All you need is a couple of pegs and a piece of string. Knock a peg into the ground at the central point, attach the string to it and then tie the second peg to the other end, ensuring that the length of the string equals the radius of your design. Pull the string taut and mark the circumference of the circle with the second peg.

To set out the structure built step-by-step on pages 46 and 47, pegs were knocked into the ground at each corner and the foundation footings marked with flour. The yellow line indicates the outside edge of the structure since the foundations are 200 mm (8 in) wider than the pillars on all sides. To check for square, a red peg has been inserted as described above. A steel tape is used to check the distance between the red peg and the corner.

BUILD YOUR OWN CARPORT AND PERGOLA 31

A facebrick pillar and screen wall match the exterior walls of the house.

BRICKS AND MORTAR

While it is quite possible to erect carports and pergolas without using brickwork anywhere, brick and block walls, piers and pillars are features which are often found in even the simplest designs.

The basic techniques required for bricklaying are reasonably easy to master, although, as with any other building techniques, it will take practice to perfect them.

Bricks and blocks

There is a wide range of bricks and blocks available which are suitable for garden structures. This includes facebricks, clay and concrete bricks designed to be plastered, inexpensive concrete blocks which are also plastered, and reconstituted (reconstructed) stone blocks made in imitation of natural stone. Although special tools and skills are required for cutting natural stone, this material may also be used.

Various bricks and blocks which are suitable for paving are discussed on pages 16 and 44.

Mortar

Both bricks and blocks are bonded together with mortar to give the structure maximum strength. While a range of suitable bonding patterns may be used for garden walls, pillars and piers are most commonly built using a stretcher bond. To achieve this bond, bricks are laid lengthways and those in each successive course overlap the bricks below by half. For the mortar you will need cement, sand (sometimes referred to as soft sand) and water. Use the same Portland cement as you do for concrete. This may be mixed with ordinary building sand (to which hydrated builder's lime should be added to improve the binding and water-retentive quality of the mixture) or plaster sand (which may already contain lime). In some areas, plasticiser is used instead of lime, and some people even use liquid soap as a substitute in small projects.

Dry premixed mortar is available too, although, like premixed concrete, it is considerably more expensive.

A suitable mix for general external use is based on a cement:sand ratio of 1:4. Combine the dry materials and add water (as though you were making concrete, but without adding stone). The mixture is ready for use when it is of a uniform colour and consistency, and when you can push a brick into it end on with your hand. It should have a plastic texture and be cohesive to achieve a good bond with the bricks.

Mix only enough mortar for immediate use. After about two hours it will start to stiffen and will have to be discarded. Never try to soften it at a later stage by adding more water as this will weaken the mixture.

Bricklaying

The most important tool you will use is a trowel, essential for lifting the mortar and buttering the bricks. In addition, you will need a spirit level and a builder's square, and you should also make a gauge rod (see page 38), which is invaluable for maintaining equal courses. For cutting bricks, use the chisel end of a brick hammer, or a bolster and hefty club hammer. If you are building with facebricks, you will also need a jointing tool to finish off the brickwork.

Before attempting to lay bricks for the first time, practice using the trowel. The technique is reasonably easy to master; the secret is to ensure that the brickwork remains square, level and plumb. For this reason it is essential to make frequent use of your spirit level, square and gauge rod (see pages 28 and 38).

32   BUILD YOUR OWN CARPORT AND PERGOLA

Each brick course is bedded in mortar, which will bond better if slightly furrowed. Butter the header (the short end) of the brick before sliding it into position; if there are any gaps, use the trowel to fill them with more mortar. Tap the brick gently into place with the trowel handle until it is level, and then scrape off any excess mortar.

Plaster or render

Unless pillars and piers have been built with facebricks, the surface should be plastered or rendered. Not only is a plaster finish decorative, but it will also make the structure more weatherproof.

Plaster or render is made in exactly the same way as mortar, but it is more important to add lime to the mixture. This helps to prevent cracking and gives the plaster or render a plastic quality, making it easier to apply. Plaster sand, which has a lime content, is therefore generally preferred.

Newly built brickwork is usually perfect for plastering; if it is dusty or grimy, clean it before work begins. It is also advisable to moisten the surface 24 hours before it is plastered or rendered to prevent too much water from being absorbed from the plaster mix.

Garage and carport walls have been plastered and painted to match the house.

Apply the plaster, or render, to the surface with a plasterer's trowel, pressing it down to ensure that it sticks. Leave it for about half an hour before scraping it to a uniform finish with a screed board; then smooth it with a wooden or steel float. Use a corner trowel to neaten the corners. Take care not to over-trowel the surface as it can bring the finer material to the surface and cause cracking. While plaster is usually 10 to 15 mm (about ½ in) thick, uneven areas may require a thicker covering. If this is necessary, apply it in two coats. Let the first set, then scratch it to provide a key for the second.

Plaster should not dry out too quickly, so keep it damp for two or three days by spraying it lightly with a hose. Once the surface has dried, you can paint it; whether you use a primer and/or sealant first depends on the paint you use and on local climatic conditions.

Plaster or render is applied to the surface with a trowel.

A simple carport with white plastered pillars, built beside a garage.

BUILD YOUR OWN CARPORT AND PERGOLA 33

TIMBER

The type of wood chosen will depend on what is available locally, what is required for your design, and cost – with forest depletion, the price of many woods has soared in recent years and some formerly common woods are now hard to find. Timber can be bought as poles or as cut wood (including laminated timber), both of which are suitable for a wide range of garden structures.

Cut timber

Both hardwoods (from deciduous trees) and softwoods (from conifers) may be used in the garden, although most woods must be treated in some way. A hardwood like teak is tough and will withstand most weather conditions, but few people can afford it; other less expensive hardwoods can be substituted. Suitable softwoods include redwood and various pines, but it is essential that they be treated for structural use.

Various preservatives are used, most of which are applied under extreme pressure, although different countries favour certain specific products. These include pentachlorophenol and tributyl tin oxide – both organic substances. Generally speaking, if a wood has been treated according to recognised specifications, it will be suitable for construction purposes and as durable as other materials.

If you are treating your own timber, do so before construction, and ensure that it is thoroughly dry, otherwise the chemicals will not penetrate.

Rough-cut wood may be used for carports, but it is generally better to opt for planed timber or laminated beams. Although the latter are more expensive, they are also stronger and more stable. Another advantage of using laminated wood is that it is available in much longer lengths, more than double the span of ordinary planks and beams. Cover strips (thin, flat strips of wood) or half-round strips of timber may also be useful for securing shadecloth and awning material in position and preventing it from lifting in heavy wind.

Never accept wood that is badly warped or cracked. While small knots are unavoidable in many woods, it is best to avoid boards with very large knots, as they can affect the strength of your structure.

While the roof structure of most buildings consists of a number of components (beams, trusses, rafters, battens and so on), the configuration of carport and pergola roofs is usually simple. Such a structure typically has beams supporting crosspieces or purlins, which in turn hold up the roof sheeting. Some structures may also have battens, which are usually smaller than purlins.

Poles

There is a charming rusticity about pergolas built with poles. Using poles does not limit the usefulness of the structure, and they may be combined with cut timber, for example, to create a more sophisticated shelter with a solid roof structure.

Usually there is a choice between poles which have simply been debarked, and those which have been machined to a smooth surface, making them reasonably regular in size. Split poles, which are useful if you wish to incorporate railings or screen a section of the pergola, are also available commercially. Whatever you choose, it is best to opt for poles that have been treated against infestation and rot.

Traditionally, hardwood poles were dipped in or coated with creosote, a dark brown oil distilled from coal tar and considered for many years to be the best wood-preservative. If it is not pressure-treated, though, it wears off and must be regularly reapplied. It is also toxic to plants and will cause some materials, including shadecloth, to rot.

Today, many sawmills impregnate poles with substances which enable the wood to resist pests and withstand damp conditions. One of the most common of these substances is chromated copper arsenate (CCA), a water-based preservative which usually gives wood a slight green tinge.

Poles that have not been treated should at least be coated at one end with a bituminous waterproofing compound, creosote or some other preservative which will prevent them from deteriorating too rapidly when buried in the ground.

Poles and rough-cut timber combine to create a rustic pergola in a Japanese-style garden.

Working with wood

One of the attractions of a wooden structure is that it is reasonably simple for the amateur to erect. The materials are comparatively easy to handle, and the carpentry skills involved are generally elementary. If you have an aptitude for making things and can use a drill and a saw, you are already halfway there.

You do not need an elaborate toolkit, and can even make a simple structure with hand tools alone. The minimum equipment you will need is a saw, steel tape measure, drill (an inexpensive hand drill will suffice), screwdriver, hammer, and of course the tools required to ensure that the poles, posts and beams are square, level and plumb (see pages 28-29). Power tools will, of course, simplify the task. If you do not have any tools, consider how much you will use them in future, as well as how much you can afford to spend, before going shopping.

Finishes

Most timber, especially softwood that has been cut and planed, needs additional protection if it is to look attractive and last for a reasonable length of time. While a good quality hardwood like teak will weather to a gentle grey colour without losing its strength and stability, softwoods like pine should always be varnished or painted. If you are planning to paint or seal your pergola or carport, ensure that the preservative you use is compatible with the finishing coat – some treatments, for instance creosote, cannot be overcoated.

Perhaps the simplest coating is a penetrating oil preservative dressing which will waterproof the wood and protect it against the weather, rot and insect attack. These dressings are easy to apply but, because they are not resistant to sunlight, have to be reapplied every six to nine months. They are also more suitable for use on hardwoods than on softwoods. Although it is not a preservative dressing as such, linseed oil will 'feed' the wood, and can be used on its own on some hardwoods.

A timber structure can easily be erected by a DIY builder.

Exterior varnish, which comes in various shades and both matt and gloss finishes, is generally UV-resistant as well as waterproof. A good quality wood varnish will last for several years.

Alternatively, you can paint the wood. There are numerous types of paint from which to choose, although the most usual kind found on outdoor structures is ordinary gloss paint, which will give you a tough, durable surface in a vast range of colours. In addition to two coats of gloss paint, you will first have to prime the wood to protect it and aid adhesion, and then give it a suitable undercoat.

OTHER MATERIALS

While brick and timber are certainly the most common materials used for the upright framework of carports and pergolas, these are by no means the only options.

Timber beams varnished for protection.

Precast concrete

A practical and attractive choice, precast concrete pillars are well suited to carports and pergolas. They are available in a variety of styles and heights, and if you wish, they may be concreted on to a precast plinth or a brick base to raise their height. These pillars usually have built-in reinforcing on to which the roof beams or poles are bolted.

BUILD YOUR OWN CARPORT AND PERGOLA 35

Metal

Galvanised steel poles are commonly used for carports, and less frequently, for pergolas. Poles should be at least 38 mm (1½ in) in diameter, and set in substantial footings (see pages 29-30) or bolted into a base plate and post connector which has been attached to a concrete slab.

Rectangular or square aluminium tubing is sometimes used for carport construction. However, it is not a common do-it-yourself material.

Fibrecement

Piping made from fibrecement is a more unusual, but quite acceptable, material. It may be used in the same way as poles, with fat pipes forming the uprights, and thinner ones the crossbeams. The uprights should be reinforced and filled with concrete.

Far left: A simple carport made from fibrecement poles.
Left: An all-metal carport.
Above: Precast concrete pillars support timber beams.

SPECIAL CONNECTORS FOR POLES

A 'Log Dog' bracket connects two poles.

'Gumbou' brackets join poles at all angles.

While regular screws and bolts are universally available and easy to use, new inventions which are specifically designed for connecting logs and poles to each other and to other components often appear on the market. These inventions can be very useful, and are worth experimenting with. The most successful connectors are often patented in several countries. In spite of their effectiveness, however, a major problem with many of them is availability, as some of the smaller manufacturers are unable to fund large-scale marketing programmes – so if you are building with poles, shop around in your area.

One of the simplest methods of joining logs and poles is to use a specially formed galvanised metal cradle. For instance, 'Log Dog' (which has been patented in the USA and Australia and which is available in several other countries) is a rigid connector which will support a range of poles varying from 90 mm (3½ in) to 140 mm (5½ in) in diameter. It has claws and spikes, as well as holes for screws or nails, all of which stabilise the structure.

Pole hangers, which are screwed to the wall and have an angled base to support the pole, are particularly useful when one

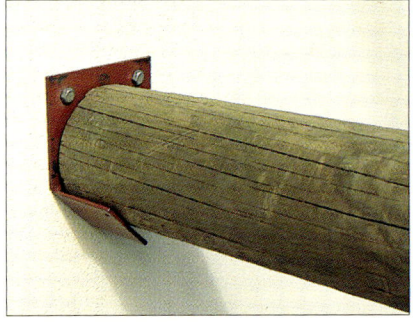

A pole hanger screwed to the wall.

is constructing a carport or pergola against a building or garden wall.

Other V-shaped connectors, some of which bolt together, are invaluable when assembling structures which do not meet at 90° angles. 'Gumbou', a South African invention, is a series of galvanised steel brackets which enable you to join poles at any angle. No drilling is required; the brackets, a spanner, a hammer and nails are all you need. The structure will be strong enough not to need concrete foundations – simply sink the poles into holes 800 mm (2 ft 8 in) deep, fill the holes with earth, and compact it thoroughly.

FIXING AND FASTENING

Numerous fastening aids are available in the building industry, including a variety of nails, truss and joist hangers, bolts, clamps, couplings, screws and rivets. While different products are recommended for different materials, aluminium, brass, stainless steel and galvanised fastenings should be used where possible as they will not rust or stain wood.

Various cuphead bolts and washers, coach screws and wire nails are essential for all projects. Crosspieces and uprights are usually bolted or screwed together, although nails can also be used. Beams can be held together with clips, grips and joist hangers. Truss hangers can be used to fix beams to a wall. Uprights can be fastened to specially manufactured post anchor bases which are attached to concrete with expanding bolts or anchor bolts. Bolts and screws should be long enough to go right through the timbers they are securing. If they are too long, they can be cut with a hacksaw once they are in place. Spiked metal connector plates, designed to simplify the assembly of roof trusses, are also useful for joining beams when the required lengths of timber are not available.

If you wish, angle iron may be adapted for attaching pieces of timber to each other or to a wall. Clamps and galvanised hoop iron are useful for securing the roof structure. Mild steel reinforcing rods are invaluable when building brick pillars.

Tacks, wire nails or heavy duty staples are used if shadecloth is chosen to provide shelter. Special fasteners with 'teeth', similar to those used to connect roof trusses on site, are also available in some areas.

Metal poles with support brackets hold the main beams in place.

Galvanised brackets are used to secure poles and the timber roof structure.

Upright poles are bolted to the main beams of this carport; purlins are slotted into notches and nailed down. (See Plan 1 on page 52).

Metal has been concreted into a precast pillar to secure the overhead beams of this pergola.

BUILD YOUR OWN CARPORT AND PERGOLA 37

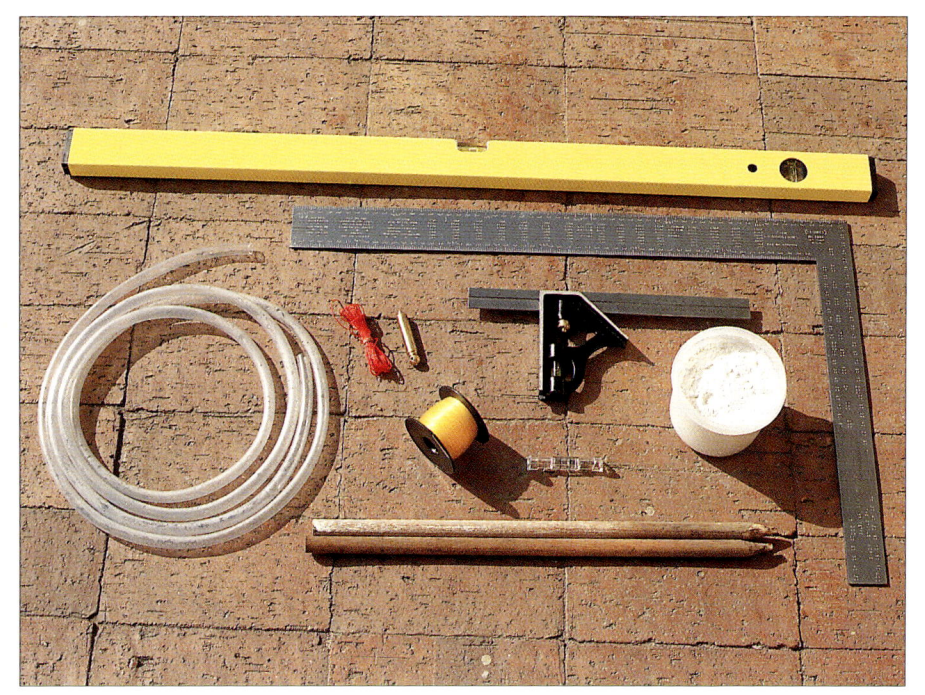

Essential tools used for setting out and levelling.

TOOLS

Do-it-yourself enthusiasts usually have a selection of tools which will be quite adequate for all of the projects described. Most are available from DIY or hardware stores, although a few will have to be made at home. If you do not want to buy new tools, they can often be hired.

Setting out and levelling

Essential equipment that you will need for setting out your site and for ensuring that your structure is square, level and plumb must be included in your basic toolkit for any building job. In addition, you will need to use a good quality retractable tape measure at all stages of the project.

Chalk is sold for setting out a site, although you could use lime or white cement instead, if you have it. Even flour can be used, and is usually the cheapest option too.

Squares are indispensable to all aspects of the building operation. A steel square and an adjustable carpenter's square are particularly useful. A home-made wooden square is practical for setting out; it can be made by nailing together three pieces of wood cut in the ratio 3:4:5 – for example, lengths of 0.9 m, 1.2 m and 1.5 m (3 ft, 4 ft and 5 ft) – to create a right-angled corner. A combination square, which incorporates a small spirit level, is handy for minor bricklaying projects and carpentry.

Pegs, used for setting out and for holding a builder's line in place, may be metal or wooden, although the latter are cheaper and are also easy to make yourself.

Builder's line or string is used for setting out, and to ensure that paving or brickwork is straight and level.

Levels are also essential for all stages of any building project, from the foundation up. They include spirit levels which are available in several lengths, home-made water levels made from transparent tubing, and line levels, which can be useful but are not essential (see pages 28-29).

Punners are ramming tools which you can make by attaching a heavy weight to the end of a pole. A punner is used instead of a compacting machine to compact earth or hardcore before paving or concreting.

Plumb bobs are for checking vertical surfaces. Simply a weight attached to a length of string, a plumb bob is not necessary for garden building projects.

Spades and shovels are used to dig foundations and mix concrete, mortar and plaster. A **pick** is also useful if you are excavating hard ground.

Concrete and brickwork

In addition to the basic tools used for levelling and for ensuring that the brickwork is square and plumb, there are a number of other items you cannot be without when working with concrete or bricks.

Wheelbarrows are essential to have for removing soil from the site and transporting materials, and are useful for mixing concrete and mortar.

Trowels are used for both bricklaying and plastering. Small pointing trowels are useful for neatening the joints of facebrick surfaces, and corner trowels (available for both inner and outer corners) are useful for giving plaster edges a neat finish.

Straightedges and gauge rods are simply lengths of wood, used to level concrete and to check the mortar joints between brick courses respectively. A gauge rod can easily be made by marking off a straight length of wood at intervals equal to one brick plus a 10 mm (½ in) mortar joint.

Corner blocks are used to string up a builder's line as bricklaying progresses. The line is wrapped around the block and through the slot to secure it, and the blocks are then hooked on to the ends of brickwork. They are also useful for checking levels and to help you ensure that pillars are square with one another. Corner blocks are sometimes available commercially, or they can easily be made by sawing a groove halfway through an L-shaped piece of wood.

Hammers with a chisel end (brick hammers) are used for cutting bricks.

38 BUILD YOUR OWN CARPORT AND PERGOLA

A selection of tools used for concrete and brickwork.

Alternatively, a club hammer may be used with a bolster. A rubber mallet, which looks like a hammer but has a heavy rubber-topped head, is used to tap pavers and slabs into position.

Bolsters (broad chisels) are useful for cutting bricks.

Jointing tools are not essential for garden brickwork. They are used for pointing or shaping the mortar joints in facebrick walls, but may be substituted with a piece of metal.

Mortarboards and screedboards are used by professional bricklayers and plasterers respectively to hold small quantities of mortar and plaster while they work.

Floats, made in both wood and metal, are used for smoothing plaster and the screed laid over concrete.

Woodwork

While power tools will simplify just about any carport or pergola project, there are some simple hand tools which you cannot afford to be without. You will also need the basic levelling tools, a good quality tape measure and a carpenter's pencil.

Saws are the first requirement in a woodworker's toolkit. However careful you are when ordering the correct lengths, there is invariably some cutting to do. While a stocky back saw or tenon saw will cope with most small jobs, a general purpose bowsaw is best for sawing logs and a hacksaw (which may also be used for cutting metal) is favoured by some do-it-yourselfers. Ripsaws, for cutting along the grain, crosscut saws which work best across the grain, smaller panel saws, which do both, and power saws are all useful.

Drills are fairly expensive, but are essential for woodwork. If you do not already own an electric drill (see page 40) and do not intend to invest in one, you could use a hand drill (a wheel brace for minor applications and a more heavy-duty bit brace are both useful) for a relatively simple construction project. Remember that you will also need the correct wood bits for the woodwork, and ordinary masonry bits for drilling into brickwork or concrete.

Screwdrivers are indispensable, and you will need the right size for the job. Sophisticated spiral ratchet screwdrivers, with different positions and a reverse action, are a worthwhile investment, but are not essential.

A range of tools required for woodwork, including a selection of saws and screwdrivers.

BUILD YOUR OWN CARPORT AND PERGOLA

Hammers are necessary for nailing pieces of wood together. With a claw hammer you will also be able to extract nails.

Spanners are needed to tighten nuts and bolts. There are several types from which to choose.

Chisels, rasps and files are useful for shaping, planing and finishing small lengths of wood, especially when jointing beams.

Power tools

Although power tools are not an essential requirement, there is no doubt that they do take the drudgery out of many jobs. They also enable you to cope with many construction problems which hand tools simply cannot manage.

Drills will simplify most projects. For joining wood, screws are more accurate and will give a more secure grip than nails, but holes must be drilled for them.

Although a single-speed drill is the cheapest option, a two-speed or variable-speed drill is more versatile and therefore a better buy, although it will obviously cost more. An electric drill with a hammer action is useful if you need to drill into really hard materials such as concrete lintels. Cordless drills, which run on batteries, are also available.

Saws are essential for cutting wood, and power saws will speed up and streamline the job. A circular saw will make smooth perpendicular or angled cuts in most materials, while a jigsaw will cut curved lines.

Planers enable you to smooth the surface of long pieces of timber at home. They may also be used for bevelling or angling edges and for cutting simple rebates.

Sanders are useful for smoothing timber which has already been planed. A belt sander will remove material quickly and is the best tool to use for levelling planks and boards; vibrating orbital sanders are better for finishing a surface which would otherwise be sanded by hand.

Other useful power tools include compactors and plate vibrators (which compact hardcore or soil for foundations or paving); angle grinders for cutting bricks and tiles; and block splitters or masonry saws for halving some precast concrete products.

Useful power tools, left to right: (top) belt sander, angle grinder, planer, orbital sander; (bottom) circular saw, two drills, jigsaw.

QUANTIFYING AND COSTING

Once you have settled on a design, you will need to work out quantities of materials required, and the cost of the project. If you choose to adapt one of the plans on pages 52-63, alter the given quantities accordingly.

Use working drawings (the drawings submitted to council) or do your own sketches to scale. The more detailed they are, the more accurately you can determine costs. List all the materials you will need, and increase quantities of bricks, cement and so on (including those listed for the plans) by about 10% to allow for wastage and breakage.

Bricks and blocks

Although brick sizes vary slightly, you can assume that 110 bricks will be enough for a square metre (11 ft²) of one-brick wall 222 mm (8¾ in) thick, and 55 bricks for half-brick or single walls.

To determine the number of bricks in a pillar, divide the planned height of the pillar by that of the brick plus mortar joint to assess how many courses you will need, then multiply by the number of bricks used in each course. A 2.4 m (7 ft 10 in) two-brick pillar, built with four 222 mm x 106 mm x 70 mm (8¾ in x 4 in x 2¾ in) stock bricks in each course and 10 mm (⅜ in) mortar joints, will use 120 bricks. If the structure has four pillars, you will need 480 bricks for the pillars.

The number of blocks needed to build a wall or pillar depends, of course, on the size of the blocks used. The blocks used for the pergola on page 62 measure 390 mm x 190 mm x 190 mm (1 ft 3 in x 7½ in x 7½ in), and about 13 of these are required for each square metre (11 ft²) of wall. If your blocks are a different size, multiply the length (plus mortar joint) in millimetres by the height (plus mortar joint) in millimetres, and divide the result into 1,000,000 (or divide the result in square inches into 1,296 – the number of square inches in a square yard). Alternatively, calculate the surface area of your proposed wall and divide by the size of one block. Apply the same principle used for bricks to work out how many blocks you will need for pillars.

Perforated decorative screen walling blocks are usually 290 mm x 290 mm x 90 mm or 100 mm (11⅜ in x 11⅜ in x 3½ in or 4 in) and you will need 11 blocks for every square metre (11 ft²).

To lay a square metre (11 ft²) of brick paving you will need about 45 pavers.

Cement
You will need cement for foundations, slabs, mortar, and plaster or render.

For major building projects one would order ready-mixed concrete according to the compressive strength required, but simple mix proportions are adequate for most garden brickwork. If you use 19 mm (¾ in) stone for foundations and footings, a cement:sand:stone mix in the ratio 1:4:4 (by volume) will yield about 5¼ units of measurement; adjust the ratio to 1:4:3 for 13.2 mm (½ in) stone, though. If you are building fairly substantial walls, a slightly stronger 1:3:4 mix is recommended for the foundations. For every cubic metre (35 ft³) of foundations you will need 4½-5 bags (225-250 kg or 505-560 lb). If you are casting a concrete floor, use a 1:2:3 mix – you will need about eight bags of cement per cubic metre (35 ft³).

If mixing by hand, it is preferable to work out quantities required per bag of cement (50 kg or 112 lb), for which you will need 150 litres (33 gal) each of sand and stone (for a 1:4:4 mix). The yield will be about 205 litres (45 gal).

When mixing mortar, you can count on using one bag for every 200 bricks in a half-brick wall, or for every 150 bricks in a one-brick wall (which has a double skin of brickwork). Mix cement with sand in the ratio 1:4 (by volume), or if lime is added, 2:1:8 for cement:lime:sand. If you are using 390 mm x 190 mm x 190 mm (1 ft 3 in x 7½ in x 7½ in) blocks, a weaker 1:6 cement:sand mixture is adequate and you will need about one bag for every 100 blocks. As you will use about 12½ blocks per square metre (11 ft²) of wall, 50 kg (112 lb) of cement should be enough to build about 8 m² (86 ft²).

The same mix ratios may be used for plaster, which will then match the strength of the mortar. It should be 10-15 mm (about ½ in) thick, and you will need about 4 kg (9 lb) of cement for every square metre (11 ft²).

Pillars are seldom left hollow, so you will need extra cement for concrete to fill in the central cavity – unless you are building solid, one-brick square piers.

Sand
Quantifying sand by volume is never very accurate because sands differ and their moisture content varies. The mass of sand per cubic metre (35 ft³) is roughly 1,350 kg (2,976 lb).

Using a 1:4 cement:sand mix for both mortar and plaster, for every 100 bricks of one-brick wall you lay you will need 100 litres (22 gal) or about 2½ 50 kg (112 lb) bags of sand. For plastering, 12 litres (2⅔ gal) or 16 kg (35 lb) will be enough for each square metre (11 ft²).

If there is a lot of brickwork and you order in bulk, a cubic metre of sand (35 ft³) is enough for laying 1,000 bricks or plastering 84 m² (900 ft²) of wall.

Sand is also required for foundations and concrete slabs. Work out the quantities for foundations according to the ratios already specified. For a slab, a 1:2:3 cement:sand:stone ratio is recommended. Alter this to 1:2:2 if you are working with the smaller stone.

Paving bricks and blocks should be laid on a layer of building sand 25-50 mm (1-2 in) thick. At a thickness of 40 mm (1½ in) (as specified in the plans on pages 52-63) one cubic metre (35 ft³) will cover 25 m² (269 ft²). You will need slightly more to brush over the surface once paving is complete (see pages 42-43). Some people advocate brushing on a 1:6 cement:sand mix instead of pure sand.

Stone
As the vital coarse aggregate used for making concrete, stone is essential for all foundations and solid slabs. The quantity will depend partly on the size of stone you use – relevant proportions are detailed above. For the designs in this book, the requirements for 19 mm (¾ in) stone have been listed.

Binders
If you use plaster sand with a lime content for mortar and plaster, no extra lime is needed. Note that adding lime to ordinary builder's sand to improve its binding quality will give a slightly higher yield if you use the same cement:sand mix proportions. Alternatively, add 50 ml (2 fl oz) of plasticiser to every 50 kg (112 lb) of cement. For small projects, use a tablespoon of good quality liquid soap as a substitute.

Timber
It is almost always cheaper to buy timber in standard lengths. Check what is available before designing your structure – or adapt the requirements to fit. If a number of smaller lengths are to be used (for a screen or railings, for instance), buy whatever lengths will give you the least wastage. If the lengths used in the plans on pages 52-63 are not available, buy longer pieces and cut to size.

Roofing materials
Many roofing materials are available in only a few standard widths. Instead of cutting the sheets (which may be difficult to handle), it is usually possible to design a structure utilising the full expanse. This simplifies construction and cuts down on time and labour.

Guttering
To ensure effective drainage, guttering is installed on structures with a solid roof covering, often on one side only, to catch the run-off from a sloping roof. Some designs include concealed gutters, adjacent to the fascia board or at the back of the structure between wall and beam. A downpipe, the length of a pillar or post, takes water from the gutter to a channel or drain. Remember to buy the correct brackets and connectors to fit these components.

Other costs
If you are planning to enlist the help of professionals or artisans, include their fee in your final costing. Rather overestimate their time, otherwise you may throw out the budget at a crucial time and jeopardise the entire project.

Budget for materials such as tiles, reinforcing and connectors, finishing touches like paint and plants, and any tools you need to buy. Add in a figure for removing excess soil and rubble.

STEP-BY-STEP GUIDE TO CONCRETE WORK

The principles of casting or throwing concrete are the same for foundations, footings and solid slabs. When you tackle a large area, the concrete should be cast in sections of up to 9 m² (97 ft²); cast alternate sections one day and the rest when the concrete has set.

MATERIALS
A basic concrete mix consists of cement, sand, stone and water. The quantities and ratio you use depend on the type of work and the area to be covered (see pages 29-30 and 41). The concrete slab of a patio or carport should be at least 100 mm (4 in) thick.

CONSTRUCTION
Formwork or shuttering
You will need to create formwork or shuttering to contain the concrete while it sets. Use timber or metal (preferably aluminium) forms, lightly oiled with a 'release agent' to prevent the concrete from sticking to them. Set out the area to be concreted as shown on page 31, with additional pegs around the edge, about 1 m (3 ft) apart. Then set up the formwork to a height corresponding to the required depth of the slab.

Cracks
If cracks develop in the slab while the concrete is still malleable, the surface can be reworked within four hours of pouring (before it sets). To repair cracks in old concrete, chip away loose material, coat the cracks with a bonding agent and patch with new concrete.

1 Start by preparing the site. Dig out the soil to a depth of about 150 mm (6 in) – or 100 mm (4 in) if hardcore is not needed – making sure that the ground is firm and level so that the concrete will settle evenly. Remove all vegetation, including roots.

2 Hardcore, or crushed stone, will provide a more stable base on a site with loose or clay soil. It may also be used to fill holes. Measure the area for the carport and spread the material evenly with a shovel to form a 50 mm (2 in) sub-base.

3 Level the surface as best you can. Fill any gaps in the sub-base with clean builder's sand, and compact it thoroughly with a punner. Alternatively, specialised equipment and machinery may be hired to simplify the job.

4 Check the level you have created using a spirit level, placed on a straightedge if necessary. You will need to allow a slight gradient of about 1:40 away from any adjacent building in order to provide effective drainage of rainwater to the trench.

5 Before you fix the formwork in place, divide the area into sections which are no more than 9 m² (97 ft²) in size. When the formwork is removed, you will be left with joints which will help prevent uncontrolled cracking of the concrete.

6 Hammer wooden or metal pegs into the ground where the corners of each section are to be. String a builder's line between them, 100 mm (4 in) above the sub-base, to mark the intended finished height of the concrete surface.

7 Now you can set up the formwork, ensuring that the top of each length corresponds with the line. Hammer pegs into the ground on either side of the formwork to keep it in place. If necessary, place wedges under the lengths to raise them.

8 Check the levels of the formwork with a spirit level, once again allowing for a slight drainage slope. The formwork must be set accurately at this stage as its top edge will determine the surface level of the concrete slab.

9 You will need a clean, dry container to measure out the required quantities of cement, sand and stone. It should be strong and rigid; a 12 litre (2½ gal) builder's bucket, an empty 25 litre (5½ gal) paint can, or a large oil drum is ideal.

10 If you are using a concrete mixer, load the stone first, together with a little water. Add the cement next and then the sand, with just enough water to make the mixture workable. If you are mixing by hand, add the stone last (see page 41).

11 Before pouring the concrete, moisten the ground to prevent the sub-base and soil from drawing water from the mixture. Transport the concrete to the site in a wheelbarrow and pour it into the section of formwork furthest from your mixing place.

12 Overfill the formwork so that the concrete is about 25 mm (1 in) above it before compaction. Use a chopping action with a straightedge or heavy wooden beam to compact the concrete and expel all air. Use a sawing motion to level it.

13 Care must be taken to work the concrete against the formwork and into all corners. If there are any hollows, these should be filled and levelled. The concrete is sufficiently compact when pasty cement and water start to come to the surface.

14 Finish the surface with a float, pressing down and using a circular movement. Since outdoor concrete should be fairly rough if it is not to become slippery in wet weather, use a wooden float to do this. A steel float will create a very smooth finish.

15 In moderate climates, formwork can usually be removed the day after the concrete is cast. Ideally, allow it to cure for five to seven days. Either cover the surface with plastic or sacking (which should be kept damp), or hose it down regularly.

BUILD YOUR OWN CARPORT AND PERGOLA 43

STEP-BY-STEP GUIDE TO BRICK PAVING

Brick paving is one of the most popular floor surfaces for patios and carports, and it is a project which all do-it-yourselfers can easily undertake.

Although paving is sometimes laid on concrete, it is often placed on a bed of sand. If you have unstable soil (such as clay), incorporate a well-compacted base of hardcore beneath the surface.

MATERIALS
The type of brick you use will depend largely on the effect you wish to create. Clay and concrete bricks or blocks are available in several colours and can be laid in various patterns. Lay the bricks on clean builder's sand, 25-50 mm (1-2 in) thick, depending on the site.

CONSTRUCTION
Edging
Some sort of edging, firmly bedded in mortar, should hold the outer edges of paving in place. Precast concrete kerbstones work well along the borders of any paved surface to be used by cars, especially if a carport is built on a street boundary. Bricks are more common around the edges of a patio floor. They can be laid to form a soldier, sailor or header course. Alternatively, strips of timber may be used or you can erect a narrow formwork around the edge and pour in a weak concrete mix. It is best to start paving at one edge – do not lay all the edges at once or you may end up with an odd-shaped space which will cause unnecessary cutting of bricks.

1 Measure the area and set out with pegs and line to define the space for the carport floor. Excavate the site to the correct depth, removing all vegetation. Make sure that the base is stable and well compacted. Spread fill or soil to level the site.

2 In some instances it may be necessary to include a hardcore sub-base. Both this and any fill must be thoroughly compacted to prevent future subsidence. You can use a punner, although it is more efficient to use a compacting machine.

3 Lay 150 micron plastic sheeting over the surface, overlapping the edges by about 150 mm (6 in). This will act as a damp-proof course and will also prevent weeds and grass from growing through gaps between the paving bricks or blocks.

PAVING PATTERNS

Pavers may be laid, with or without joints, in a variety of patterns – your choice depending on the effect you wish to create. Stretcher bond, which creates the pattern found in a stretcher bond wall, is one of the simplest. The various basketweave patterns are particularly attractive, and a herringbone pattern (laid diagonally or at 90° to the edging) is the best choice for a driveway as the bricks lock into each other, forming a stable surface. Other patterns include stack bond (or Jack-on-Jack), Flemish and English bond which are both laid in the same way as the equivalent wall bonds, and a variety of circular designs.

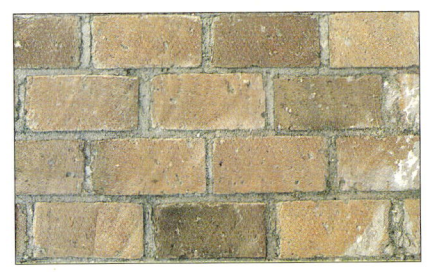

Stretcher bond

Basketweave

Herringbone

44 BUILD YOUR OWN CARPORT AND PERGOLA

4 Spread 30-50 mm (1-2 in) of clean builder's sand over the plastic. Although river sand is often quite clean, it is advisable not to use unwashed beach, dune or pit sand as these tend to contain salt, shell particles or excessive amounts of clay.

5 Smooth the sand by drawing a straightedge across it. Keep checking your levels with a spirit level placed on top of the straightedge to ensure that there is a 1:40 gradient. This will allow for drainage away from any adjacent buildings.

6 If the paving is to abut a wall, start laying from this point; alternatively, begin at an edging (see page 44). Work systematically inwards, using a steel square from time to time to ensure that the pattern is square and even.

7 Press the pavers into the sand to create the design of your choice (in this instance, basketweave). Unless you want a mortar joint, abut the bricks and gently tap each one into position with a rubber mallet. Use a spirit level to check that they are level.

8 If any brick is below the level of the paving, lift it out and pack a little extra sand in underneath. Replace the brick and tap it with the mallet to bed it into place. If a brick is too high, remove some of the sand before putting it back in place.

9 Inevitably there will be bricks which have to be cut. You can do this by scoring a clean cutting line on all four sides with a bolster, then hitting the tool with a club hammer to break it. Alternatively, you can use the chisel end of a brick hammer.

10 Once you have laid all the pavers, check the levels again. If any of the bricks protrude slightly, lay a straight plank across the surface and hammer with the mallet to flatten them. Do not hammer the bricks themselves or you may dislodge them.

11 To fill any slight gaps between the pavers, sweep a weak 1:6 cement:sand mixture over the surface with a stiff bristled brush. Although sand alone may be used, the cement will improve bonding and help to ensure that all the bricks stay in place.

12 Use a garden hose to spray the entire area lightly with clean water. If any mortar remains on the surface, gently squeegee the bricks to remove it. Allow the cement to set thoroughly – for at least 48 hours – before driving on the paving.

BUILD YOUR OWN CARPORT AND PERGOLA 45

STEP-BY-STEP GUIDE TO BUILDING A CARPORT

For a carport to offer maximum shelter, it must have a solid roof covering, and uprights must be sturdy to support a reasonably substantial roof structure.

MATERIALS
Pillars can be built of bricks or blocks; here, 390 mm x 190 mm x 190 mm (15 in x 7½ in x 7½ in) hollow concrete blocks were used. The front pillars are 2.4 m (8 ft) high, with 26 blocks in each. The back two are one block higher (28 in each) to give a 1:25 slope to the roof. You will also need concrete for the footings and mortar and plaster for the pillars. See pages 29 and 41 for a guide to proportions and quantities.

Cut and planed timber is a common choice for the roof structure. The timber dimensions depend on the size of the carport – this one is 6 m x 3.5 m (20 ft x 11 ft 9 in). The roof structure is made of standard planed timber. Beams are 6.6 m (21 ft 6 in) long and 231 mm x 69 mm (9 in x 2¾ in) in section. The seven purlins are 3.6 m (11 ft 9 in) long and 144 mm x 44 mm (5½ in x 1¾ in) across. You will also need scrap timber to brace the beams while installing the roof structure. Fibreglass sheeting covers the roof structure.

Galvanised strapping for fastening the beams is concreted into the pillars. Purlins are attached to the beams with truss hangers which are secured with coach screws and hexagonal bolts; roof sheeting is attached with roofing screws. PVC guttering and a downpipe complete the design.

1 Set out the site (see page 31), ensuring that the layout is square. Dig four 800 mm x 800 mm (2 ft 8 in x 2 ft 8 in) foundation footings at least 400 mm (1 ft 4 in) deep. Knock a peg into the centre of each to indicate the upper level of the concrete.

2 Pour the concrete mixture into each hole to the height of the peg. Allow to set overnight. At the outer corner of each pillar, set up a profile by knocking a batten or similar piece of wood into the ground. Check that it is plumb with the planned block surface.

3 Using corner blocks, set up a line between two of the profiles. Position the first course of blocks without mortar and use a steel square to check the angles. Mark off the upright timber to form a gauge rod, including a 10 mm (⅜ in) mortar joint.

4 Starting about 1 m (3 ft) from the ground, mark off a gauge on each of the other three profiles, using a water level (see page 29) to ensure that the blockwork will be level. If you are working alone, use tape to hold the water level to the profiles.

5 Mix mortar as described on page 32 and then, using a trowel, place a small amount on top of the concrete foundation. Now lay the first block, pushing it firmly into the mortar and levelling it with the first line marked on your gauge rod.

6 Lay two blocks side by side, alternating the direction for each course. Put mortar onto the surface of the block, then tap the next one into place with the trowel handle. Keep checking both horizontal and vertical surfaces with a spirit level as you work.

BUILD YOUR OWN CARPORT AND PERGOLA

| 7 | When you have laid about six courses, fill in the holes in the blocks with a weak concrete mix. If you are building brick pillars, use metal reinforcing to strengthen the structure. This is held in place with concrete or mortar which fills the central cavity.

| 8 | Continue laying until the pillar is about 2.4 m (7 ft 9 in) high. Insert a length of galvanised strapping or hoop iron into one of the holes (preferably that at the outermost corner), and fill up the cavities in the blocks with concrete as before.

| 9 | You can plaster the pillars now or once the roof structure has been assembled (see page 33). Using a combination square, measure and mark the positions of the seven purlins on the two side beams; this is where you will attach the truss hangers.

| 10 | Still working on the ground, mark the position of the coach screws on the beams and drill holes at these points. Ensure that the truss hangers are accurately positioned, then fix to the timber. Use a spanner or ratchet to tighten the screws.

| 11 | When the mortar in the pillars is completely dry, place the beams across them. Brace with battens, ensuring that the distance between them is constant and that they are level and plumb. Hammer the strapping to fit over the beams and nail it down.

| 12 | Carefully lower the purlins into position. If your measuring has been accurate, you will not have any problems, and the timber crosspieces will slot in quite easily. If necessary you can hammer the ends gently to force them into the truss hangers.

| 13 | Check that each of the purlins is level. If any of them seem to sag or are slightly lower on one side, wedge a piece of wood between the timber and the truss hanger until they are level. This is absolutely essential if roof sheeting is to be used.

| 14 | Place the roof sheeting on the purlins and drill holes in the upper section of the fibreglass profile where it covers the timber. If a join is required, overlap the sheeting. Hammer 65 mm (2½ in) roofing screws into each hole to secure the sheeting.

| 15 | The slope you have created will ensure that rainwater drains off the structure towards the gutter, which is fixed to the lowest purlin with brackets and clout nails. Connect the gutter to the downpipe with an outlet fitting and use swan necks to angle it.

BUILD YOUR OWN CARPORT AND PERGOLA

STEP-BY-STEP GUIDE TO BUILDING A PERGOLA

One of the simplest methods of building a pergola is to use treated wooden poles. These are relatively inexpensive, easy to handle and quick to erect, even if you are working single-handed.

The dimensions and exact quantities of materials you use will depend on the size of the pergola you plan to build. A materials list, detailed drawing and description of the design featured here appear on page 58.

Of course, wooden poles may be used in conjunction with other materials too. For instance, you could modify the design by replacing the uprights as shown here with brick or block pillars (see pages 32-33); or you could combine poles with a planed timber roof structure (see plan on page 52).

Any suitable floor material may be used, although brick paving, the material chosen for the floor of this pergola, is one of the most popular. Paving can be laid in a variety of patterns, although the basic techniques, as illustrated on pages 44-45, are the same. Other flooring options are suggested on pages 16-18. The roof covering – if any – will depend on the degree of shelter you require. The choice for this patio is shadecloth, which offers some protection from sun and hail, but not from rain. Other types of awning material, split poles, or even planting, could be used as alternatives. (See also pages 19-21 for a fuller range of overhead cover options.)

MATERIALS

The most important material you will need is obviously the poles which form the basic pergola structure. Select thicker poles, about 120 mm (5 in) in diameter, for the uprights, and thinner ones, about 90 mm (3½ in) in diameter, for the crosspieces which form the roof structure. Split poles should be used for the railings which partially enclose built-in seating.

In addition, you will need a standard concrete mix (see page 29) for the foundation footings. A reasonably weak 1:4:4 mixture of cement, sand and stone is quite adequate, the total quantities required depending on the design of your structure. If you are mixing a low-strength concrete by hand, using 19 mm (¾ in) stone, each 500 mm x 500 mm x 500 mm (1 ft 8 in x 1 ft 8 in x 1 ft 8 in) footing will take about half a bag of cement, two 50 kg (112 lb) bags of sand and approximately two bags or 90 kg (200 lb) of stone. If smaller stone (13.2 mm or ½ in) is used, you will need less (about 65 kg or 144 lb is more than enough).

If you plan to use shadecloth or any other kind of awning fabric to provide shade, you will need to buy enough to cover the roof structure, bearing in mind that it is sold in standard widths. Do not use shadecloth with wood which has been treated with creosote, as the creosote will rot the shadecloth fibres.

Of course, uprights and crosspieces will have to be connected to each other. A variety of cuphead bolts and washers, coach screws and clout nails are indispensable to the project; alternatively you can use one of the connectors manufactured specially for use with poles (see page 36). Wire nails, tacks, heavy duty staples or shadecloth fasteners will also be necessary if this material is used. Timber cover strips are useful for keeping shadecloth taut while you attach it to the structure.

1 Measure out the area where the pergola is to be sited and hammer pegs into the soil at the places where the poles are to be sunk into the ground. This particular structure will measure approximately 4 m x 3 m (13 ft x 10 ft) when complete.

2 Using chalk, white cement, lime or flour, mark out the position of the seven footings required. A wooden peg marks the central point of the 500 mm x 500 mm (1 ft 8 in x 1 ft 8 in) foundation area of each footing. All angles must be at 90°.

3 Remove the pegs and dig each hole to about 500 mm (1 ft 8 in). If there is grass where you are to build, remove the sods carefully for use elsewhere. Some of the sand can be used to top up the hole once the concrete has been thrown.

48 BUILD YOUR OWN CARPORT AND PERGOLA

4 Now position the seven upright poles in the holes and brace them with battens or any other suitable timber. Use a spirit level to check that all the poles are absolutely vertical, or you will end up with a lopsided structure.

5 Using a builder's bucket or any other clean, dry container of a suitable size, measure out a 1:4:4 mixture of cement, sand and stone. You can mix the materials on any clean, flat surface, although a wheelbarrow is also suitable for small batches.

6 Once the dry materials are thoroughly combined, use a spade or shovel to form a crater in the centre and slowly pour water into it, shovelling from the edges. As you turn the materials over, gradually add more water until you have a workable mix.

7 Dampen the earth in each hole slightly, and then shovel the concrete mixture around each pole, taking care not to knock it out of place. Check that all the uprights are vertical before the concrete dries and you remove the battens.

8 Use a home-made water level (see page 29) to ensure that the tops of the uprights are at the same height. Take one end of the tubing and attach it to the top of one pole; hold the other end against a second pole and mark the level of the water.

9 Repeat to level each pole, then saw the ends of the poles off at the points which you marked. As the lengths of the poles and depths of the footings may vary a little, and as the ground may slope, you may need to saw more off some than others.

10 Measure 135 mm (5¼ in) from the top of each upright pole (so that the top of the upper crossbeam will be level with the top of the pole). Using a 12 mm (½ in) drill bit, drill holes precisely where the three crossbeams are to be attached to the uprights.

11 Cut the three crossbeams to exactly the same length, and ensure that the five poles to be placed across them are also the same length as each other. This way you will not need to cut any of the beams once they have been bolted into place.

12 Measure between the points where the crosspieces and crossbeams will be bolted on. Drill holes in the crossbeams and two outer crosspieces. Measure the spacing of the crossbeams and drill three holes in each remaining crosspiece.

BUILD YOUR OWN CARPORT AND PERGOLA 49

13 Position the holes in the ends of each crossbeam in line with the holes in the corresponding uprights. With a ratchet or shifting spanner, bolt the crossbeams to the uprights, using 12 mm x 230 mm (½ in x 9 in) cuphead bolts with nuts and washers.

14 On either side of the structure, bolt a crosspiece horizontally to the inner side of the uprights, using the same size bolts. Secure the remaining crosspieces from above, using 10 mm x 200 mm (⅜ in x 8 in) cuphead bolts – hammer in, and tighten with a spanner.

15 Cut the split poles to size, either perpendicularly or forming a 45° angle at the ends which join at a corner. Although you can use one of several types of handsaw to cut the wood, an electric jigsaw makes the task easier and quicker.

16 Attach the top railing about 800 mm (2 ft 8 in) from the ground. You can pre-drill the poles as before, or drill them *in situ*. Use an 8 mm (¼ in) drill bit and mark the bit with tape at about 75 mm (3 in) to indicate the depth of the hole required.

17 Use 8 mm x 100 mm (¼ in x 4 in) coach screws to secure the railings to the pergola structure. Knock these in part of the way with a hammer and then screw into place with a shifting spanner. Use a spirit level to check that the timber is vertical.

18 Measure the required distance between the split pole railings, using a steel tape measure. Knock in nails where the bottom of each pole will be; these will help to balance the poles and keep them in place while you drill holes to attach them to the uprights.

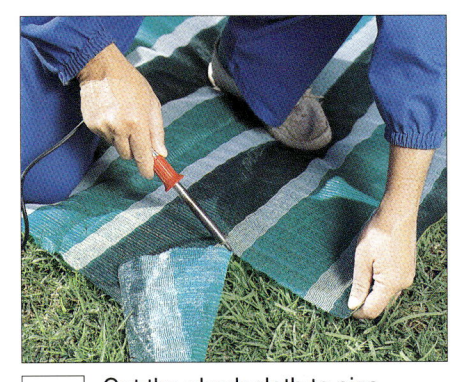

19 Cut the shadecloth to size with a soldering iron; the heat seals the edges which might otherwise fray. If you need to fasten two pieces together, use the manufacturer's monofilament or twine which will not deteriorate in sunlight.

20 Wrap one end of the shadecloth around a cover strip or other narrow length of timber, and tack or staple. This will help to keep it taut and in place. With the length of shadecloth on the underside, nail the cover strip to the poles on one side of the structure.

21 Staple the other end around a second strip of timber, and use this to fit the material tightly across the structure. Secure the shadecloth where it covers each pole. As the edges tend to sag slightly, neaten by fixing cover strips to the two remaining sides.

A concrete floor is practical for this double carport (see pages 42-43).

Brick paving in this carport matches the driveway (see pages 44-45).

The carport pillars and roof timbers are painted and an adjacent area planted (see pages 46-47).

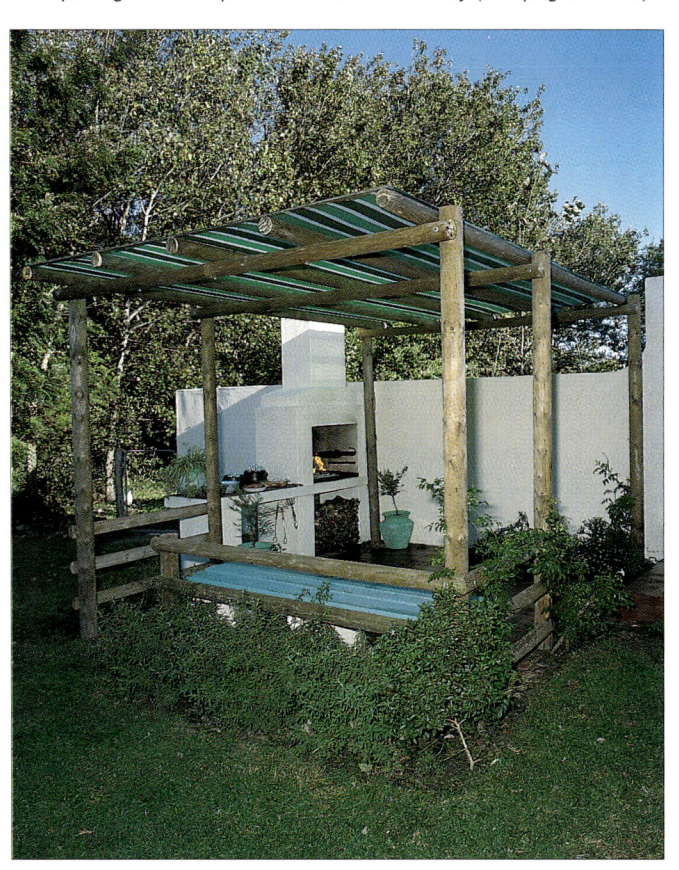

The completed pergola provides a shady spot for entertaining alongside a barbecue (see pages 48-50).

BUILD YOUR OWN CARPORT AND PERGOLA 51

DESIGNS AND PLANS

The twelve plans that follow will help you to build a variety of structures to shelter your car or shade your patio. Each comprises a checklist of materials, simple instructions, and photographs and illustrations of the finished design. Alternatively, you may prefer to create a unique carport or pergola, using ideas from several projects.

PLAN 1 — WOOD ON WOOD

Wooden poles combine with planed timber to create an attractive, free-standing carport which will suit a range of homes and add character to the surrounding garden. The fibreglass roof gives protection from sun, rain and snow.

MATERIALS

Foundations for poles
115 kg (254 lb) cement
465 kg or 0.35 m³ (1,025 lb or 12½ ft³) sand
465 kg or 0.35 m³ (1,025 lb or 12½ ft³) stone

Framework
4 x 3 m (10 ft) upright poles, 100 mm (4 in) in diameter
2 x 7 m x 228 mm x 50 mm (23 ft x 9 in x 2 in) beams
6 x 3.8 m x 75 mm x 50 mm (12 ft 6 in x 3 in x 2 in) purlins
2 x 3.8 m x 114 mm x 32 mm (12 ft 6 in x 4½ in x 1¼ in) fascia boards
8 x 75 mm x 50 mm x 50 mm (3 in x 2 in x 2 in) timber blocks

Roofing
fibreglass sheets to cover 21 m² (225 ft²)

Guttering
1 x 3 m (10 ft) PVC gutter with round channel
1 x 2.5 m (8 ft 3 in) PVC downpipe
1 gutter outlet
6 gutter brackets
2 stop ends
2 downpipe brackets
1 downpipe shoe
2 swan necks
clout nails or screws

Fasteners
8 x 12 mm (½ in) cuphead bolts with nuts and washers
40 x 8 mm (¼ in) coach screws
clout nails
roofing screws

Paving
945 bricks/blocks
1,215 kg or 0.9 m³ (2,678 lb or 32 ft³) sand

1 Dig four foundations, 500 mm x 500 mm x 500 mm (1 ft 8 in x 1 ft 8 in x 1 ft 8 in) set out as illustrated.
2 Brace poles in position, ensuring that the two back ones are slightly higher for drainage. Pour concrete into holes.
3 Saw out six notches 50 mm (2 in) wide and about 60 mm (2⅜ in) deep at 1.37 m (4 ft 5 in) intervals along both beams. Cut first and last notches 50 mm (2 in) in from ends of each beam.
4 Secure beams to poles with cuphead bolts (see detail photograph). Slot purlins into notches, then nail down.
5 Line up four wooden blocks with ends of beams and attach to outside of each end purlin with coach screws (see detail photograph). Screw fascia boards to blocks and beam ends.
6 Fix roof sheeting to the structure with roofing screws.
7 Attach gutter and downpipe to the front of the carport.
8 Pave the parking area.

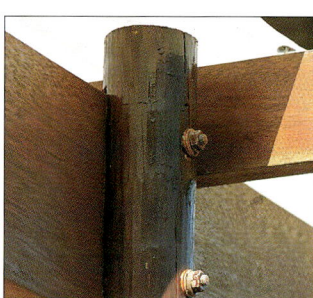

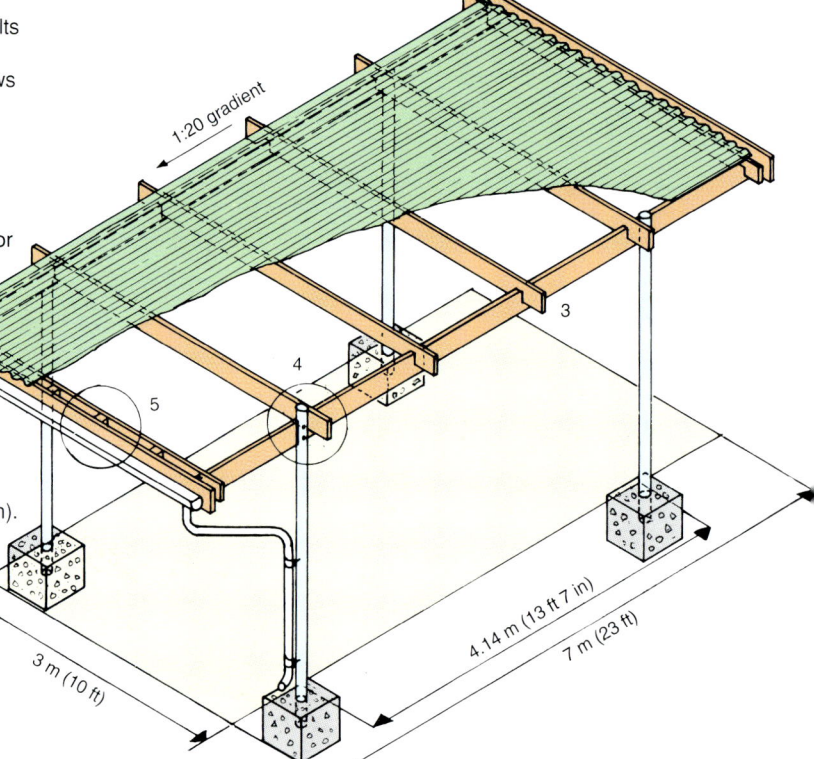

52 BUILD YOUR OWN CARPORT AND PERGOLA

PLAN 2 — POPULAR PRECAST

Six precast concrete pillars form the basis of this attractive yet simple and inexpensive carport. For stability, the pillars are concreted into the ground and three crossbeams are secured with hoop iron. Corrugated fibreglass, fixed at a slight slope, is used as a roof covering. A gutter is attached along one side, and a downpipe is secured to a short pole which is sunk into the ground.

MATERIALS

Foundations (if necessary)
40 kg (88 lb) cement
160 kg (350 lb) sand
160 kg (350 lb) stone

Framework
6 x 2.1 m (7 ft) precast pillars
3 x 3.3 m x 165 mm x 60 mm
 (11 ft x 6½ in x 2⅜ in) beams
5 x 4.64 m x 68 mm x 45 mm
 (15 ft x 2½ in x 1¾ in) purlins
2 x 4.64 m x 170 mm x 20 mm
 (15 ft x 6½ in x ¾ in) fascia boards
2 x 3.3 m x 210 mm x 20 mm
 (11 ft x 8 in x ¾ in) fascia boards

Roofing
fibreglass sheets to cover
 15.3 m² (166 ft²)

Guttering
1 x 4.5 m (14 ft 9 in) PVC gutter; square channel
1 x 2 m (6 ft 6 in) PVC downpipe
1 x 2.5 m (8 ft) pole
1 gutter outlet
4 gutter brackets
2 stop ends
2 downpipe brackets
1 downpipe shoe

Fasteners
8 mm (¼ in) coach screws
5 m (16 ft 6 in) galvanised strapping or hoop iron
roofing screws
clout nails or screws

Paving
690 bricks/blocks
810 kg or 0.6 m³ (1,786 lb or 22 ft³) sand

1 Level the area, allowing for a slight drainage slope across the width of the carport.
2 If the area is already paved or concreted, simply stand pillars on some mortar as indicated. Otherwise, prepare a shallow foundation and set pillars in place on a bed of mortar (see detail photograph).
3 Concrete strapping into the centre of each pillar. Allow to set before placing the three beams across tops of pillars. Secure with strapping.
4 Skew-nail purlins across beams at intervals of 825 mm (2 ft 9 in).
5 Fix fascia board to all sides with coach screws.
6 Fix roof sheeting in place with roofing screws.
7 Attach gutter to the back fascia board with brackets (see detail photograph).
8 Set pole in the ground at rear left-hand corner of structure. Secure downpipe to it with clout nails or screws.
9 Pave the carport floor.

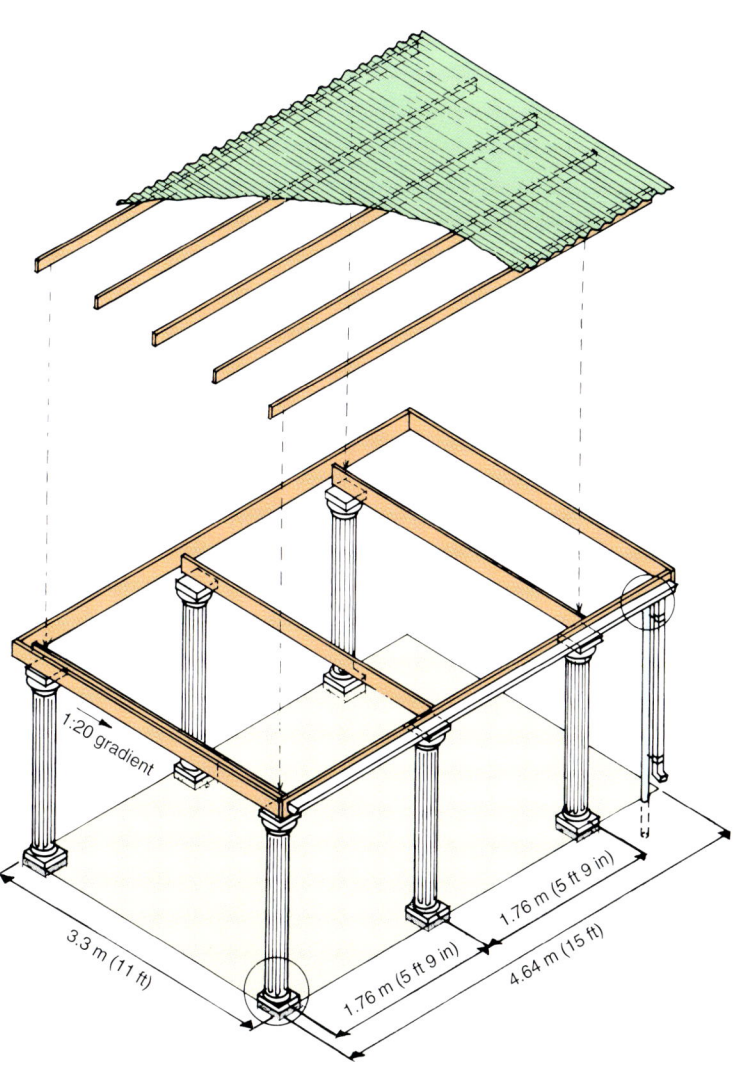

PLAN 3 — CARPORT FOR SHADE

This inexpensive all-wood structure is a perfect project for the keen amateur carpenter who needs a shady place for a car, and it can be erected in a few hours. Shadecloth nailed to the simple roof structure protects the car from the sun, snow and hail, although any other suitable awning fabric could be substituted. An attractive planter on one side doubles as a protective wall.

MATERIALS

Foundations for timber uprights
300 kg (660 lb) cement
1,215 kg or 0.9 m³ (2,678 lb or 32 ft³) sand
1,215 kg or 0.9 m³ (2,678 lb or 32 ft³) stone

Foundations for planter
40 kg (88 lb) cement
124 kg (273 lb) or 0.1 m³ (3 ft³) sand
162 kg (357 lb) or 0.1 m³ (3 ft³) stone

Framework
12 x 2.45 m x 93 mm x 22 mm (8 ft x 3½ in x 1 in) upright timbers
2 x 6 m x 152 mm x 50 mm (20 ft x 6 in x 2 in) side beams
2 x 3.82 m x 152 mm x 50 mm (12 ft 6 in x 6 in x 2 in) crossbeams
3 x 3.72 m x 118 mm x 38 mm (12 ft 2 in x 4½ in x 1½ in) purlins
4 x 3 m x 38 mm x 38 mm (10 ft x 1½ in x 1½ in) battens
6 x 1 m x 93 mm x 50 mm (3 ft 3 in x 3½ in x 2 in) timber spacers
6 x 150 mm x 93 mm x 50 mm (6 in x 3½ in x 2 in) timber spacer blocks

Planter
700 bricks
275 kg (606 lb) cement
1,114 kg or 0.8 m³ (2,456 lb or 28 ft³) plaster sand

Roof covering
shadecloth or awning fabric to cover 23 m² (250 ft²)

Fasteners
18 x 12 mm (½ in) cuphead bolts with nuts and washers
20 x 8 mm (¼ in) coach screws
10 x 12 mm (½ in) coach screws
heavy duty staples or clout nails
wire nails

Paving
1,035 bricks/blocks
0.9 m³ (32 ft³) sand

1 The planter can be built before the carport. Dig a foundation 100 mm (4 in) deep, 6.4 m (21 ft) long and 600 mm (2 ft) wide. Pour the concrete. Build half-brick walls, leaving outer wall two courses lower than inner wall. Plaster or render the surface.
2 Dig six foundations, 600 mm x 600 mm x 600 mm (2 ft x 2 ft x 2 ft).
3 Pour the concrete. Push the long spacers into the wet concrete and allow it to set.
4 Bolt uprights together in pairs with the smaller spacers placed halfway up. Slot over the blocks set in concrete and secure each with two cuphead bolts (see detail photographs).
5 Now begin assembling the roof structure, securing side beams to four corner uprights with 8 mm (¼ in) coach screws, one from each side.
6 Cut about 45 mm (1¾ in) off a purlin, to fit the structure, and attach 38 mm (1½ in) below top of middle pairs of uprights with 12 mm (½ in) coach screws.
7 Nail crossbeams to front and back of the structure.
8 Slot the two remaining purlins into place, halfway between central purlin and crossbeams. Secure as before, using 12 mm (½ in) coach screws.
9 Nail battens into place, skew-nailing where they join above middle purlin.
10 Staple or nail shadecloth or awning fabric to timbers.
11 Pave the carport surface.

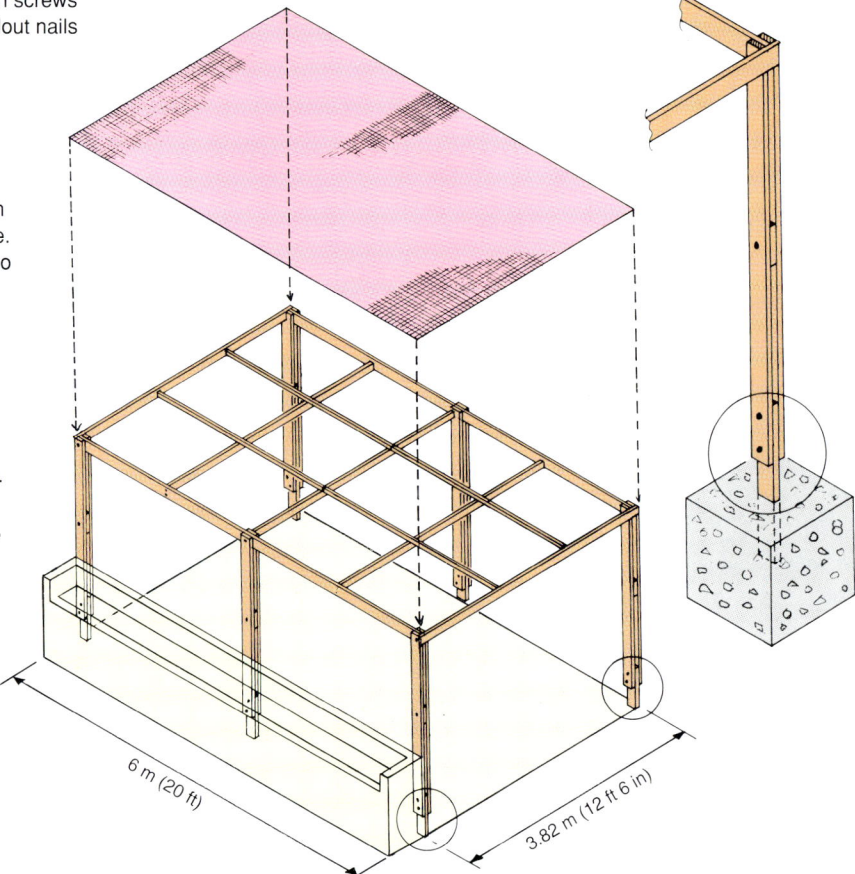

54 BUILD YOUR OWN CARPORT AND PERGOLA

PLAN 4   SIMPLY SINGLE

This single carport will suit many house styles. It is a solid yet simple structure, designed to fit in front of an existing garage, although it could be freestanding if two more metal poles were used. The roof slopes slightly, away from the existing building, and a concealed gutter is attached to a downpipe which leads to a rainwater channel. In very windy areas you should use thicker poles than those specified.

MATERIALS

Foundations for poles
100 kg (220 lb) cement
405 kg or 0.3 m³ (893 lb or 11 ft³) sand
405 kg or 0.3 m³ (893 lb or 11 ft³) stone

Concrete floor
500 kg (1100 lb) cement
0.75 m³ (26 ft³) sand
1.2 m³ (42 ft³) stone

Framework
2 metal poles, 76 mm (3 in) in diameter, with main-beam support brackets attached
2 x 5 m x 152 mm x 76 mm (16 ft 5 in x 6 in x 3 in) beams
1 x 3 m x 152 mm x 76 mm (10 ft x 6 in x 3 in) beam
4 x 3 m x 114 mm x 50 mm (10 ft x 4½ in x 2 in) rafters
1 x 3 m x 76 mm x 50 mm (10 ft x 3 in x 2 in) purlin
2 x 5.1 m x 152 mm x 38 mm (16 ft 9 in x 6 in x 1½ in) fascia boards
1 x 3.3 m x 152 mm x 38 mm (10 ft 10 in x 6 in x 1½ in) fascia board

Roofing
fibreglass sheets to cover 15 m² (162 ft²)

Guttering
1 x 3 m (10 ft) PVC gutter with round channel
1 x 2.5 m (8 ft 3 in) PVC downpipe
1 gutter outlet
4 gutter brackets
2 stop ends
2 downpipe brackets
1 downpipe shoe
2 swan necks
clout nails or screws
precast rainwater channel (optional)

Fasteners
4 x 12 mm (½ in) Rawl bolts
10 x 100 mm x 50 mm x 50 mm (4 in x 2 in x 2 in) galvanised angle brackets, 3 mm (⅛ in) thick
53 x 8 mm (¼ in) coach screws
clout nails
6 x 4.5 mm (⅛ in) self-tapping screws
roofing screws

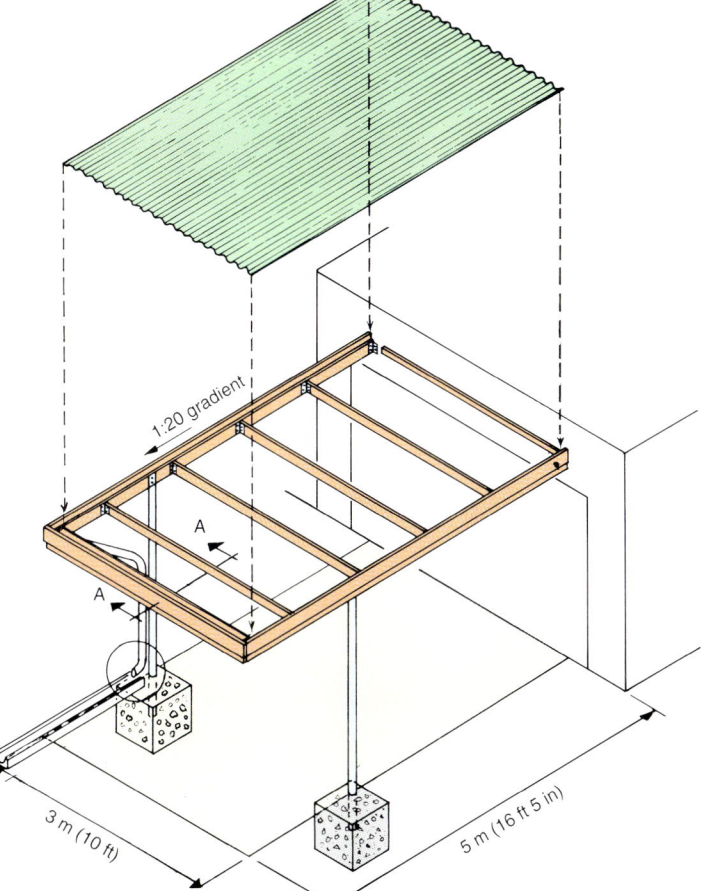

1 Dig two foundations, 600 mm x 600 mm x 600 mm (2 ft x 2 ft x 2 ft).
2 Set poles in concrete, brace and allow concrete to set.
3 Cast concrete slab, either now or when the structure is complete.
4 Fix purlin to wall with angle brackets and Rawl bolts, allowing for a slight drainage slope.
5 Using coach screws, attach longer beams to angle brackets and to support brackets at tops of poles. Attach shorter beam between side beams at the front of the structure.
6 Working from back of the structure, attach rafters to beams, fixing an angle bracket to each side of the rafter at both ends for added stability.
7 Nail gutter brackets to inside surface of front beam and attach gutter (see detail sketch).
8 Screw fascia boards to structure on all three sides, concealing guttering.
9 Fix roof sheeting to structure with roofing screws.

BUILD YOUR OWN CARPORT AND PERGOLA   55

PLAN 5   SLATE SOPHISTICATION

This double carport was designed to be attached to the front of a garage. Its framework consists of two brick pillars with a wooden roof structure bolted on to the garage wall. Corrugated iron sheeting has been used for maximum protection, while guttering is concealed between the wall and the carport. The appearance of this structure has been enhanced by fixing slate tiles to the beams to match the roof of the adjacent house. For security and practicality, a light was fitted after construction.

MATERIALS
Foundations for pillars
90 kg (200 lb) cement
365 kg or 0.3 m³ (805 lb or 11 ft³) sand
365 kg or 0.3 m³ (805 lb or 11 ft³) stone

Framework
360 facebricks
90 kg (200 lb) cement
50 kg (112 lb) lime
365 kg or 0.3 m³ (805 lb or 11 ft³) sand
extra cement, sand and stone for concrete to fill pillar cavity
2 x 2.4 m (8 ft) reinforcing rods
2 x 6 m x 297 mm x 50 mm (20 ft x 12 in x 2 in) beams
4 x 6.2 m 297 mm x 70 mm (20 ft 4 in x 12 in x 2½ in) rafters

Roofing
corrugated iron sheeting to cover 38 m² (410 ft²)
72 x 350 mm x 260 mm (1 ft 2 in x 10 in) slate tiles

Guttering
1 x 6.2 m (20 ft 4 in) PVC gutter with square channel
1 x 2 m (6 ft 6 in) PVC downpipe
1 gutter outlet
5 gutter brackets
2 stop ends
2 downpipe brackets
1 downpipe shoe
clout nails or screws
precast concrete channel

Fasteners
8 x 200 mm x 80 mm x 80 mm (8 in x 3 in x 3 in) galvanised angle brackets, 3 mm (⅛ in) thick
50 x 8 mm (¼ in) coach screws
2 wall plates
10 anchor bolts
clout nails
roofing screws
hoop iron

Paving
1,512 bricks/blocks
1.3 m³ (46 ft³) sand

1 Dig two foundations, 800 mm x 800 mm x 300 mm (2 ft 8 in x 2 ft 8 in x 12 in).
2 Pour concrete into holes and leave to set overnight.
3 Build pillars to a height of 2.4 m (8 ft), building hoop iron into the centre for last five courses. Allow mortar to set thoroughly.
4 Bolt wall plates to wall opposite pillars, but slightly lower to allow for drainage slope.
5 Screw angle brackets on to beams at equal intervals, leaving a gap at one end for concealed gutter. Fix beams in place so that they extend over outer edges of pillars, securing with hoop iron.
6 Attach guttering to one of the rafters and fix between beams (see detail illustration and photograph).
7 Working away from the wall, position rafters and screw in place.
8 Fix roof sheeting to the structure with roofing screws.
9 Use clout nails to fix tiles to outside of exposed beams.
10 Pave the parking area.

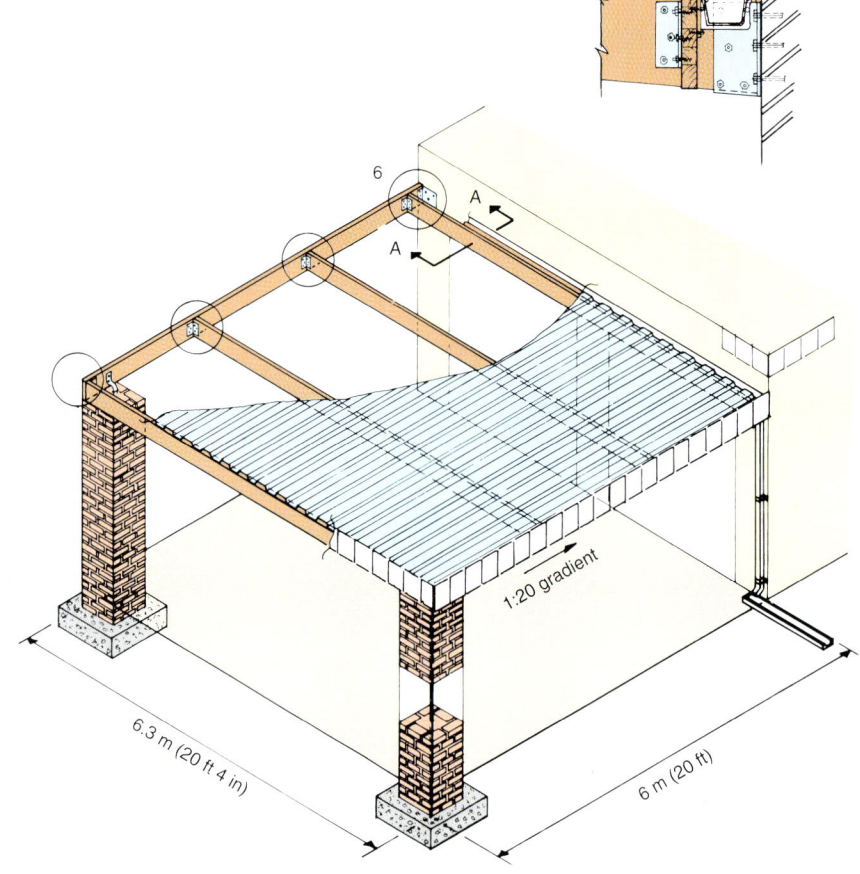

BUILD YOUR OWN CARPORT AND PERGOLA

PLAN 6   CLEVER COMBINATION

With good planning, a carport can double as a storage area for garden tools. This brick structure incorporates a small, windowless shed at one end, behind the carport wall. A low retaining wall is included in the design because the site slopes, although for flat sites this would not be necessary. While a thorough knowledge of bricklaying is required for this project, you do not have to be a professional to tackle it.

MATERIALS

Foundations for pillars and walls (including storeroom)
700 kg (1,550 lb) cement
2.1 m³ (73 ft³) sand
2.1 m³ (73 ft³) stone

Brickwork
5,250 bricks
2,000 kg (4,409 lb) cement
2 m³ (70 ft³) plaster sand
extra cement, sand and stone to fill cavity in pillars
4 x 2.4 m (8 ft) reinforcing rods
2 airbricks

Roof structure
2 x 7.8 m x 278 mm x 50 mm (25 ft 6 in x 11 in x 2 in) beams
6 x 6 m x 278 mm x 50 mm (20 ft x 11 in x 2 in) purlins
2 x 7.8 m x 278 mm x 30 mm (25 ft 6 in x 11 in x 1 in) fascia boards
1 x 6 m x 278 mm x 30 mm (20 ft x 11 in x 1 in) fascia board

Roofing
corrugated steel sheeting to cover 36 m² and 5.64 m² (390 ft² and 60 ft²)
fibreglass sheeting with matching corrugation to cover 5.64 m² (60ft²)

Guttering
1 x 6 m (20 ft) PVC or fibrecement gutter with round channel
1 x 2.3 m (7 ft 6 in) PVC or fibrecement downpipe
1 gutter outlet
5 gutter brackets
2 stop ends
2 downpipe brackets
1 downpipe shoe
clout nails or screws

Fasteners
clout nails
roofing screws
hoop iron

Floor
1,800 kg (3,970 lb) cement
2.7 m³ (95 ft³) sand
4 m³ (140 ft³) stone

Additional items
DPC (made of 250 micron PVC) to cover about 12 m² (130 ft²)
1 door
1 door handle
2 door hinges
screws

1 Dig two pillar foundations, 700 mm x 700 mm x 250 mm (2 ft 4 in x 2 ft 4 in x 10 in). Dig strip foundations for walls, 700 mm (2 ft 4 in) wide and 250 mm (10 in) deep, length as indicated.
2 Pour concrete into foundations and cast slab; allow to set for 24-48 hours.
3 Build pillars to a height of about 2.4 m (8 ft), reinforcing with rods from foundation level. Build hoop iron into last five courses.
4 Build retaining wall and shed according to plan with hoop iron at corners of shed. Front pillars should be slightly lower than back wall of shed to allow for drainage. Construct outside walls with a cavity and build in airbricks directly opposite each other. Allow mortar to set thoroughly before assembling roof structure.
5 Fix beams in place with hoop iron. Saw out notches 50 mm (2 in) wide and 228 mm (9 in) deep at ends of purlins and slot into position at equal intervals along the structure (see detail sketch). Nail down.
6 Nail fascia boards to three sides of the structure.
7 Fix corrugated iron sheeting to beams over carport; alternate iron and fibreglass sheeting over shed.
8 Attach gutter and downpipe to beam at the front of the structure.

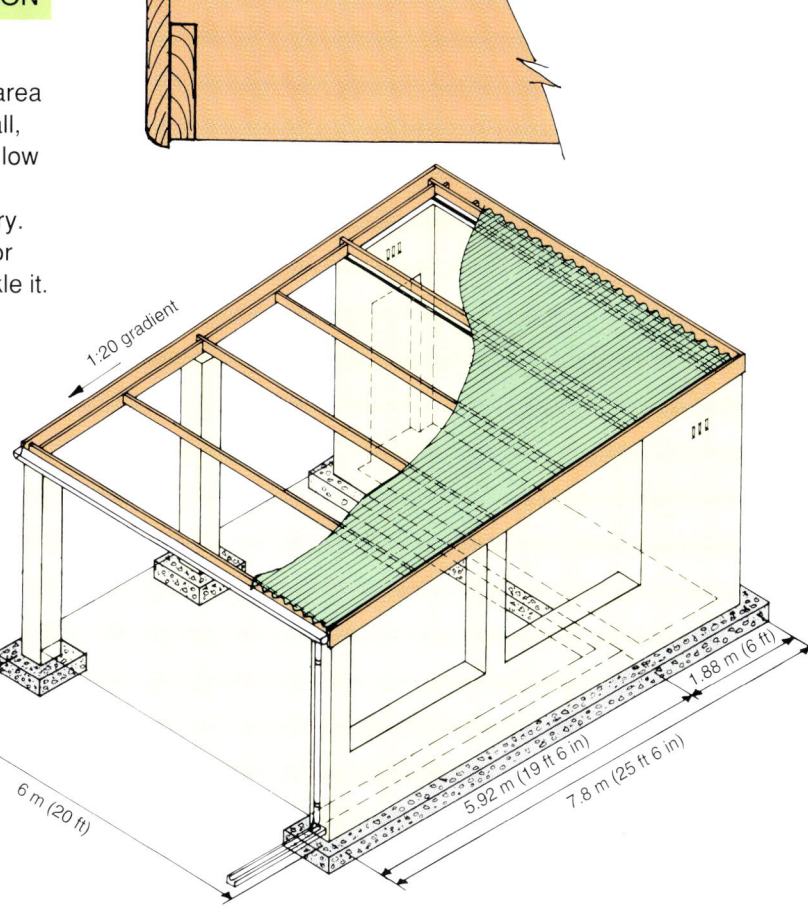

BUILD YOUR OWN CARPORT AND PERGOLA   57

PLAN 7   EASY POLE PERGOLA

This charming, easy-to-build pergola is the perfect structure to cover a simple barbecue patio. Striped shadecloth shelters the area from the hot summer sun, while brick paving underfoot makes it a practical place for entertaining. A simple bench, easily added to the design, is partially screened by a rustic split-pole railing which can also serve as a climbing frame for creepers.

MATERIALS

Foundations for poles
230 kg (507 lb) cement
930 kg or 0.7 m³ (2,050 lb or 25 ft³) sand
930 kg or 0.7 m³ (2,050 lb or 25 ft³) stone

Framework
6 x 3 m (10 ft) upright poles, 120 mm (5 in) in diameter
1 x 1.25 m (4 ft) upright pole, 120 mm (5 in) in diameter
3 x 3.25 m (10 ft 6 in) beams, 90 mm (3½ in) in diameter
5 x 4 m (13 ft) crosspieces, 90 mm (3½ in) in diameter
3 x 2.3 m (7 ft 6 in) split poles, 45 mm (1¾ in) in diameter
6 x 1.4 m (4 ft 6 in) split poles, 45 mm (1¾ in) in diameter

2 x 3 m x 45 mm x 10 mm (10 ft x 1¾ in x ⅜ in) cover strips
2 x 4 m x 45 mm x 10 mm (13 ft x 1¾ in x ⅜ in) cover strips

Roof covering
shadecloth to cover 12 m² (130 ft²)

Fasteners
12 x 12 mm (½ in) cuphead bolts with nuts and washers
9 x 10 mm (⅜ in) cuphead bolts with nuts and washers
18 x 8 mm (¼ in) coach screws
clout nails
heavy-duty staples and tacks

Paving
540 bricks/blocks
675 kg or 0.5 m³ (1,488 lb or 17½ ft³) sand

1 Dig seven foundations, 500 mm x 500 mm x 500 mm (1 ft 8 in x 1 ft 8 in x 1 ft 8 in) set out as illustrated.
2 Brace poles in position. Pour concrete into holes.
3 Ensure that tops of taller poles are level. Bolt the beams to them, 135 mm (5¼ in) from top with 12 mm (½ in) cuphead bolts.
4 Using 12 mm (½ in) cuphead bolts, secure a crosspiece on either side of structure, allowing an overhang of about 200 mm (8 in) at each end.
5 Position remaining three crosspieces over beams at intervals of 730 mm (2 ft 5 in). Secure from above with 10 mm (⅜ in) cuphead bolts.
6 Attach railings with coach screws.
7 Nail sides of shadecloth to the 4 m (13 ft) lengths of cover strip; stretch over structure and staple along crosspieces. Tack to the 3 m (10 ft) lengths of cover strip along sides to neaten (see detail photograph).
8 Pave the surface area.

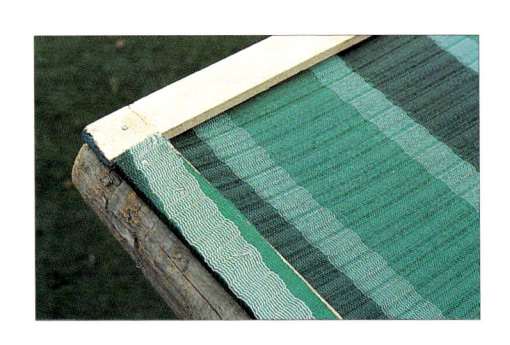

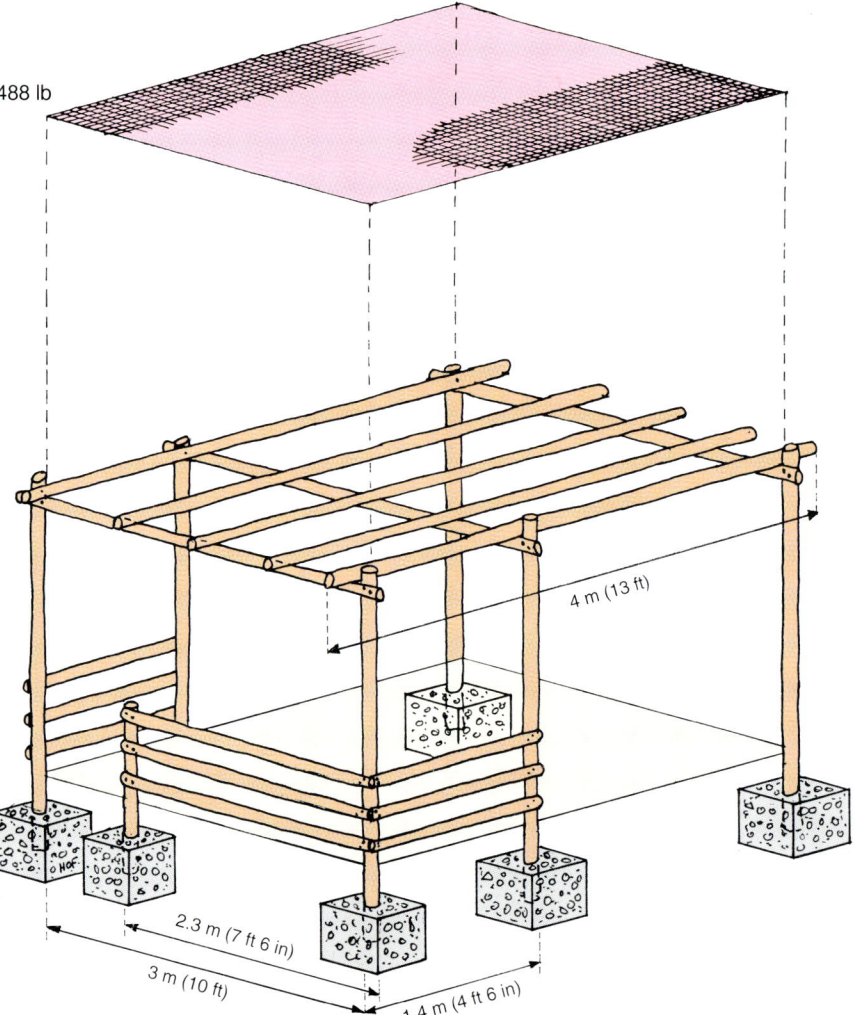

58   BUILD YOUR OWN CARPORT AND PERGOLA

PLAN 8   PRECAST PERFECTION

A blank wall alongside a swimming pool is given character by the addition of this pergola. Paint adds colour, while a lush cover of plants provides shade. Wooden cut-outs of the pillars have been attached to the wall to create a trompe l'oeil effect. Although the structure shown here is set on a substantial concrete slab and raised above the pool area, the 100 mm (4 in) slab specified in the plan is not as deep as the one depicted in the photograph. How deep you make the slab will depend on the site and your preferences.

MATERIALS
Floor
1,080 kg (2,381 lb) cement
1.6 m³ (56 ft³) sand
2.4 m³ (85 ft³) stone

Framework
4 x 2.7 m (8 ft 6 in) pillars
1 x 10 m x 122 mm x 38 mm (33 ft x 5 in x 1½ in) beam
7 x 3.2 m x 122 mm x 38 mm (10 ft 6 in x 5 in x 1½ in) crossbeams

wood for cut-outs of pillars (optional)

Roof covering
fencing wire to cover 7.5 m² (81 ft²) (optional)
4 suitable climbing plants

Fasteners
7 x 50 mm (2 in) truss hangers
14 x 8 mm (¼ in) Rawl bolts
4 x 12 mm (½ in) galvanised bolts
wire nails

1 Measure out site and throw slab. Allow to set. Finish with a screed if desired.
2 Cement pillars into place along outer edge, 2.7 m (9 ft) from wall.
3 Cut both ends of beam and one end of each crossbeam to form an attractive profile.
4 Saw out seven notches 61 mm (2½ in) deep and 38 mm (1½ in) wide in beam, 500 mm (1 ft 9 in) from each end and 1.45 m (4 ft 9 in) apart. Drill 12 mm (½ in) holes in centre of each notch.
5 Concrete galvanised bolts into tops of pillars, leaving 122 mm (4¾ in) of each bolt exposed. Allow concrete to set, then lower beam onto bolts, with notches facing upwards, and secure it.
6 With Rawl bolts, attach truss hangers to wall, exactly opposite notches in beam.
7 Saw out a notch 61 mm x 38 mm (2½ in x 1½ in) in each crossbeam, 500 mm (1 ft 10 in) from one end; drill holes as before. Slot crossbeams into truss hangers and into notches in beam, so that bolts go through holes.
8 Fix fencing wire across structure with wire nails to support plants.
9 Cut out four pillar shapes, 2.7 m (8 ft 10 in) high and screw to wall. Paint to match pillars.

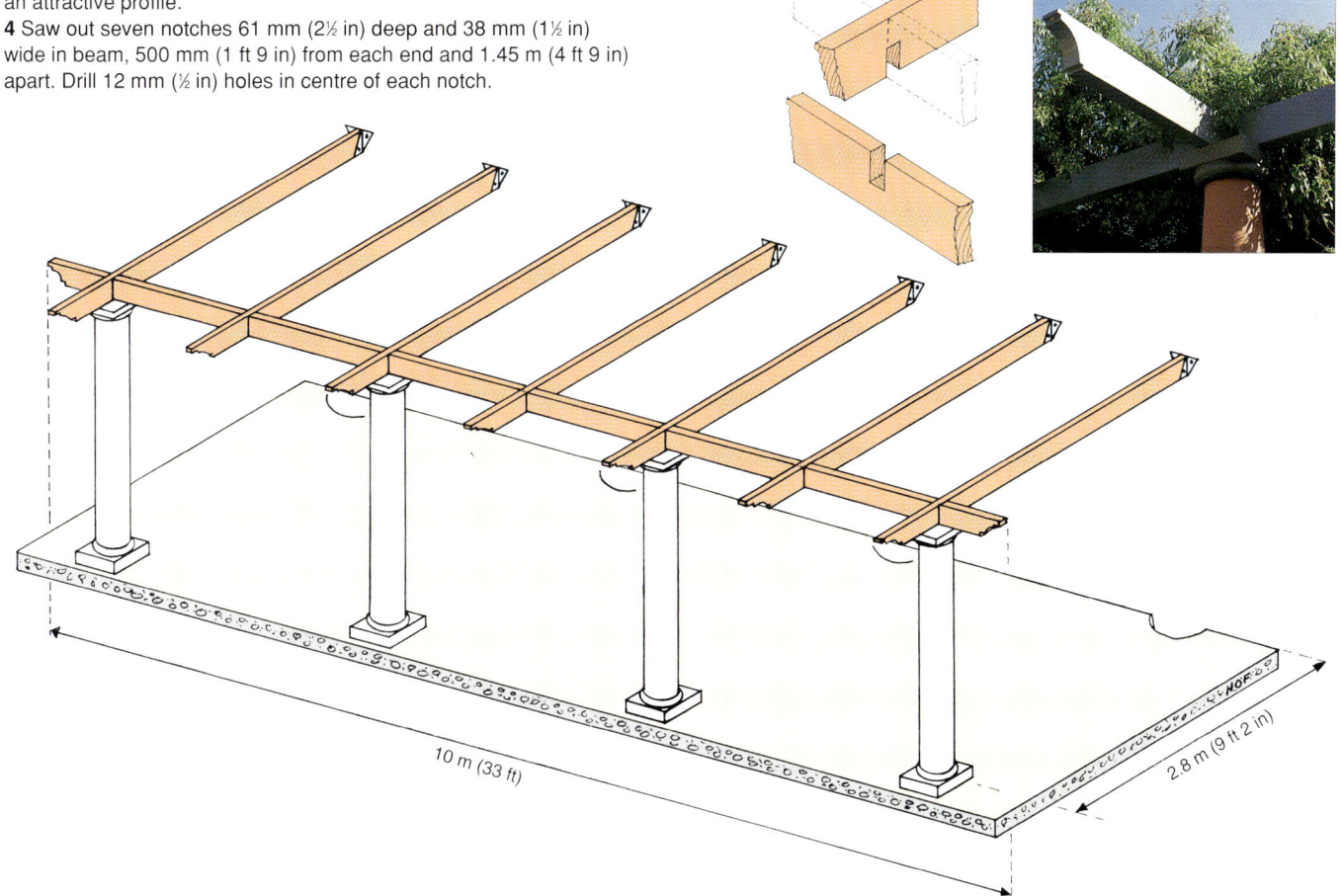

10 m (33 ft)
2.8 m (9 ft 2 in)

BUILD YOUR OWN CARPORT AND PERGOLA   59

PLAN 9 — CUT-WOOD CREATION

This elaborate, cut-wood pergola is decorative rather than functional, although it does offer a stable support for climbing plants. Designed to fit over a courtyard patio, it has been painted white to blend with the house. Although the decorative detail appears intricate, anyone with basic carpentry skills and patience will be able to tackle this project.

MATERIALS
Foundations for posts
127 kg (280 lb) cement
514 kg (1,133 lb) sand
514 kg (1,133 lb) stone

Framework
16 x 3 m x 144 mm x 44 mm (10 ft x 5½ in x 1¾ in) upright posts
8 x 3 m x 144 mm x 44 mm (10 ft x 5½ in x 1¾ in) beams
4 x 5 m x 144 mm x 44 mm (16 ft 5 in x 5½ in x 1¾ in) beams
5 x 5 m x 69 mm x 32 mm (16 ft 5 in x 2¾ in x 1 in) purlins
8 x 144 mm x 144 mm x 44 mm (5½ in x 5½ in x 1¾ in) timber spacers
8 x 222 mm x 144 mm x 44 mm (9 in x 5½ in x 1¾ in) timber spacers
extra timber for decorative detail, 69 mm x 32 mm (2¾ in x 1 in) in section

Fasteners
16 x 550 mm (1 ft 10 in) post anchors
16 x 12 mm (½ in) cuphead bolts with nuts and washers
32 x 10 mm (⅜ in) cuphead bolts with nuts and washers
40 x 12 mm (½ in) coach screws
wire nails

Paving
675 paving bricks
2 m³ (70 ft³) sand

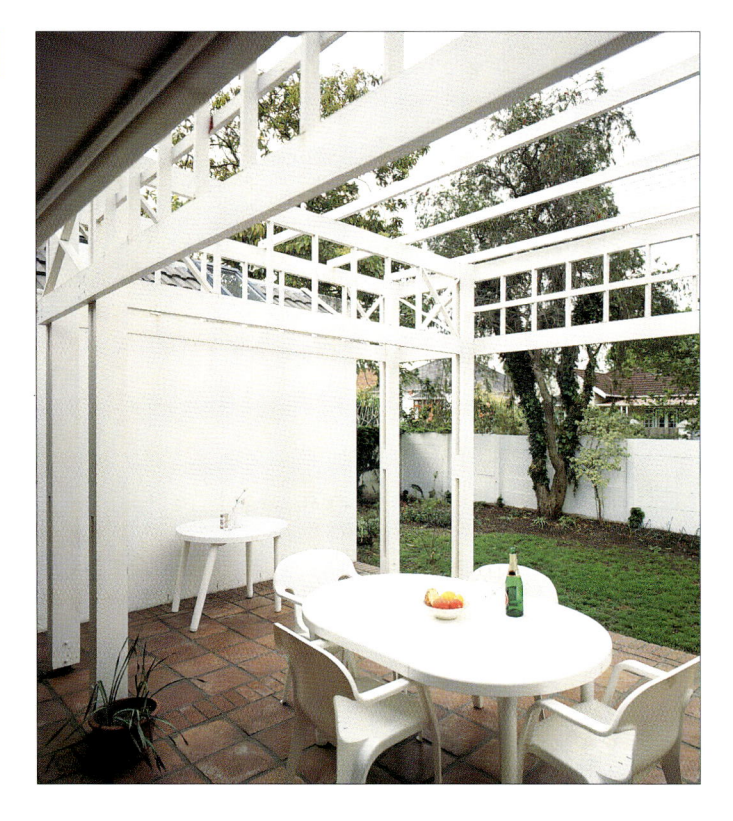

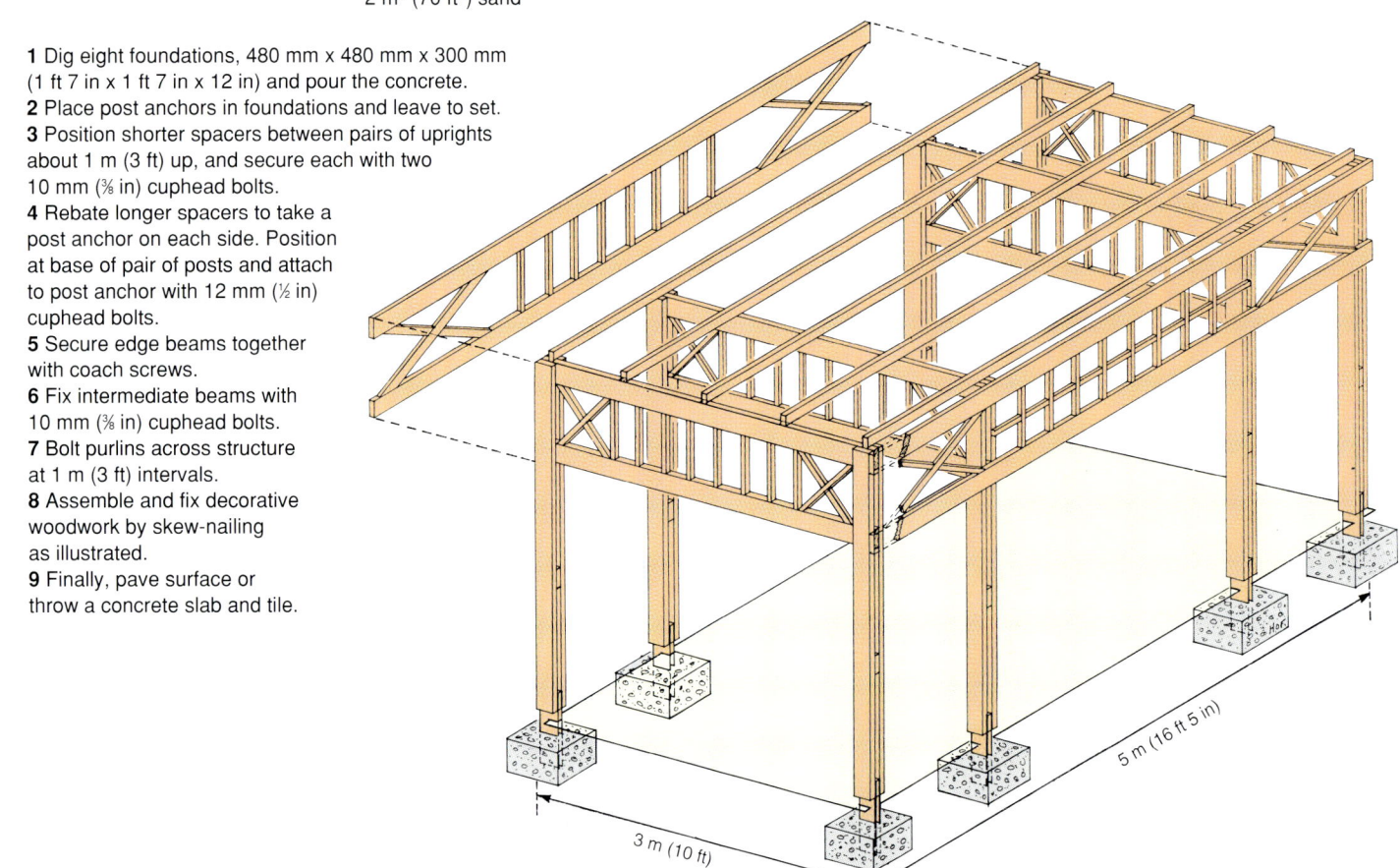

1 Dig eight foundations, 480 mm x 480 mm x 300 mm (1 ft 7 in x 1 ft 7 in x 12 in) and pour the concrete.
2 Place post anchors in foundations and leave to set.
3 Position shorter spacers between pairs of uprights about 1 m (3 ft) up, and secure each with two 10 mm (⅜ in) cuphead bolts.
4 Rebate longer spacers to take a post anchor on each side. Position at base of pair of posts and attach to post anchor with 12 mm (½ in) cuphead bolts.
5 Secure edge beams together with coach screws.
6 Fix intermediate beams with 10 mm (⅜ in) cuphead bolts.
7 Bolt purlins across structure at 1 m (3 ft) intervals.
8 Assemble and fix decorative woodwork by skew-nailing as illustrated.
9 Finally, pave surface or throw a concrete slab and tile.

60 BUILD YOUR OWN CARPORT AND PERGOLA

PLAN 10 — PERIOD-STYLE PERGOLA

Period-style poles give this attractive, slatted pergola a Victorian feel. Attached to a stone retaining wall, this unpretentious structure shades a simple barbecue and stone seat overlooking a swimming pool. While old cast-iron may be used, the poles specified are made of aluminium cast in the traditional mode. Adding two extra poles and another beam would enable it to be freestanding.

MATERIALS
Foundation footings
22 kg (49 lb) cement
89 kg (196 lb) sand
89 kg (196 lb) stone

Framework
2 x 2.4 m (7 ft 9 in) period-style aluminium poles
1 x 3.7 m x 110 mm x 32 mm (12 ft x 4½ in x 1¼ in) beam
3 x 2.7 m x 110 mm x 32 mm (8 ft 9 in x 4½ in x 1¼ in) crossbeams
34 x 4 m x 22 mm x 35 mm (13 ft x 1 in x 1⅜ in) slats

Fasteners
4 x 10 mm (⅜ in) Rawl bolts
6 x 8 mm (¼ in) Rawl bolts
4 x 8 mm (¼ in) coach screws
3 x 38 mm (1½ in) truss hangers
wire nails

Paving
300 bricks/blocks
350 kg or 0.25 m³ (774 lb or 9 ft³) sand

1 Dig two foundations, 400 mm x 400 mm x 300 mm (1 ft 4 in x 1 ft 4 in x 12 in), 3 m (10 ft) apart.
2 Pour concrete and allow to set.
3 Attach flange of poles to footings with 10 mm (⅜ in) Rawl bolts. If using old cast-iron poles, secure them in a little mortar.
4 Cut three slots, 55 mm (2¼ in) deep and 32 mm (1¼ in) wide, in main beam – in the centre and 350 mm (1 ft 2 in) from each end. Cut one slot 500 mm (1 ft 8 in) from one end of each crossbeam. Saw ends of beams to give a decorative finish.
5 Secure crossbeams to poles with coach screws.
6 Attach truss hangers to wall opposite poles and in centre of structure using 8 mm (¼ in) Rawl bolts. Slot crossbeams into place so that they fit into truss hangers and slots in main beam (see detail photograph).
7 Skew-nail slats across beams.
8 Pave the surface.

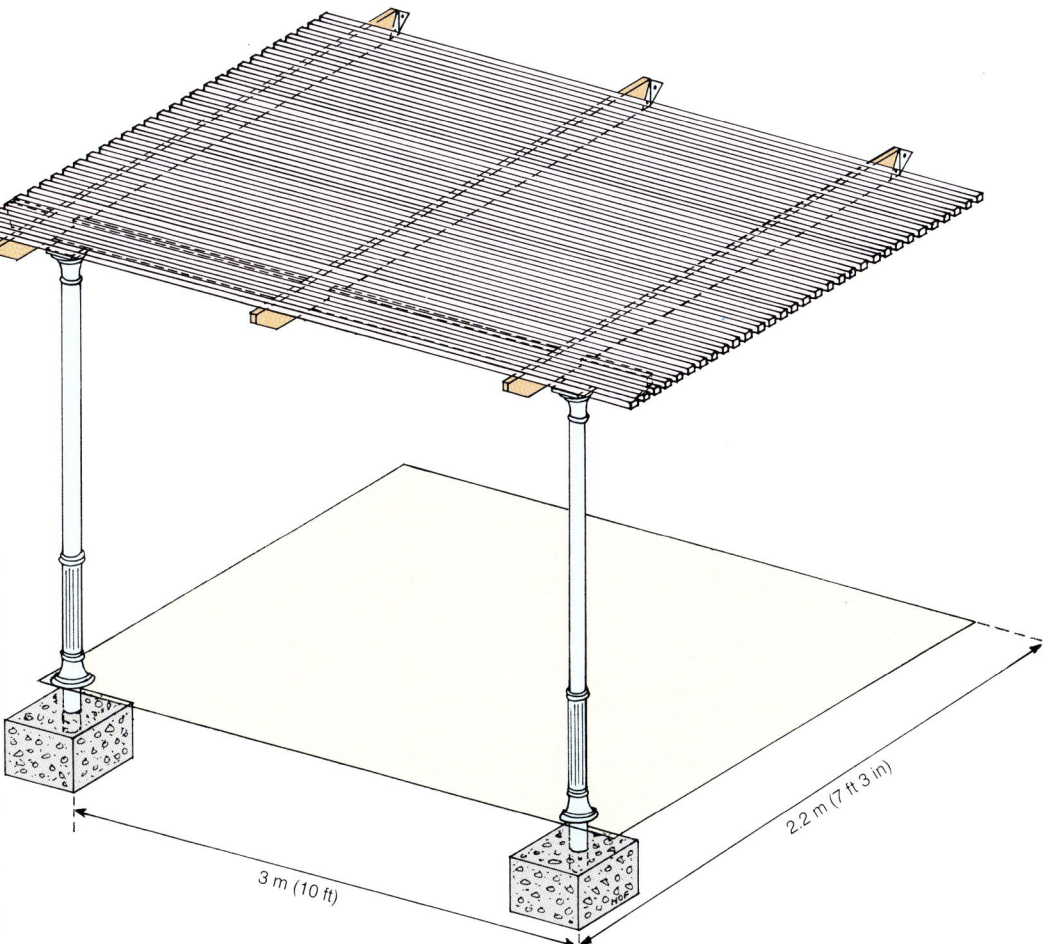

BUILD YOUR OWN CARPORT AND PERGOLA 61

PLAN 11 — PORCH PERGOLA

Sturdy brick pillars built on a substantial plinth give form and architectural continuity to a simple pergola built over the front entrance of a house. While plants form the roof covering in this case, shadecloth or awning fabric would be an appropriate alternative. Although a concrete slab was cast to level the ground before the surface was paved, this is not included in the specifications.

MATERIALS

Foundations for pillars
168 kg (370 lb) cement
680 kg or 0.5 m³ (1,500 lb or 18 ft³) sand
680 kg or 0.5 m³ (1,500 lb or 18 ft³) stone

Pillars
40 x 390 mm x 190 mm x 190 mm (1 ft 4 in x 7½ in x 7½ in) blocks
2 x 2.4 m (8 ft) threaded reinforcing rods with nuts
96 concrete bricks
220 kg (485 lb) cement
0.7 m³ (25 ft³) plaster sand
extra cement, sand and stone to fill in pillars

Roof structure
2 x 4 m x 224 mm x 44 mm (13 ft x 11 in x 1¾ in) beams
2 x 3.5 m x 224 mm x 44 mm (11 ft 6 in x 11 in x 1¾ in) crossbeams
3 x 3.5 m x 144 mm x 44 mm (11 ft 6 in x 6 in x 1¾ in) rafters
5 x 4 m x 44 mm x 22 mm (13 ft x 1¾ in x 1 in) purlins

Fasteners
3 x 12 mm (½ in) Rawl bolts
31 x 12 mm (½ in) brass countersunk screws

Paving
630 paving bricks/blocks
0.6 m³ (21 ft³) sand

1 Dig two foundations, 900 mm x 900 mm x 450 mm (3 ft x 3 ft x 1 ft 6 in) with centre points 4 m (13 ft) apart.
2 Pour concrete into holes and leave to set overnight.
3 Lay blocks to form two 5-course plinths using four blocks per course. Insert reinforcing rod and fill central cavity with concrete.
4 Build up pillars using bricks.
5 Attach beam to wall with Rawl bolts.
6 Drill a hole in one end of each crossbeam to accommodate reinforcing rods.
7 Build second beam and crossbeams into brickwork at top of pillar, painting ends with bitumen and slotting the crossbeams on to reinforcing rods.
8 Secure beam to rods with nuts.
9 Skew-nail crossbeams to beam on pillars. Attach them to beam against wall with a butt joint, using three screws at each end to secure the joint.
10 Fill cavity in pillars with concrete. Plaster pillars once mortar has set.
11 Attach rafters to beams at 1 m (3 ft 3 in) intervals, using mortise-and-tenon joints.
12 Space purlins evenly across rafters and screw into position at each end, and from the top where the purlins and rafters meet.
13 Pave the area.

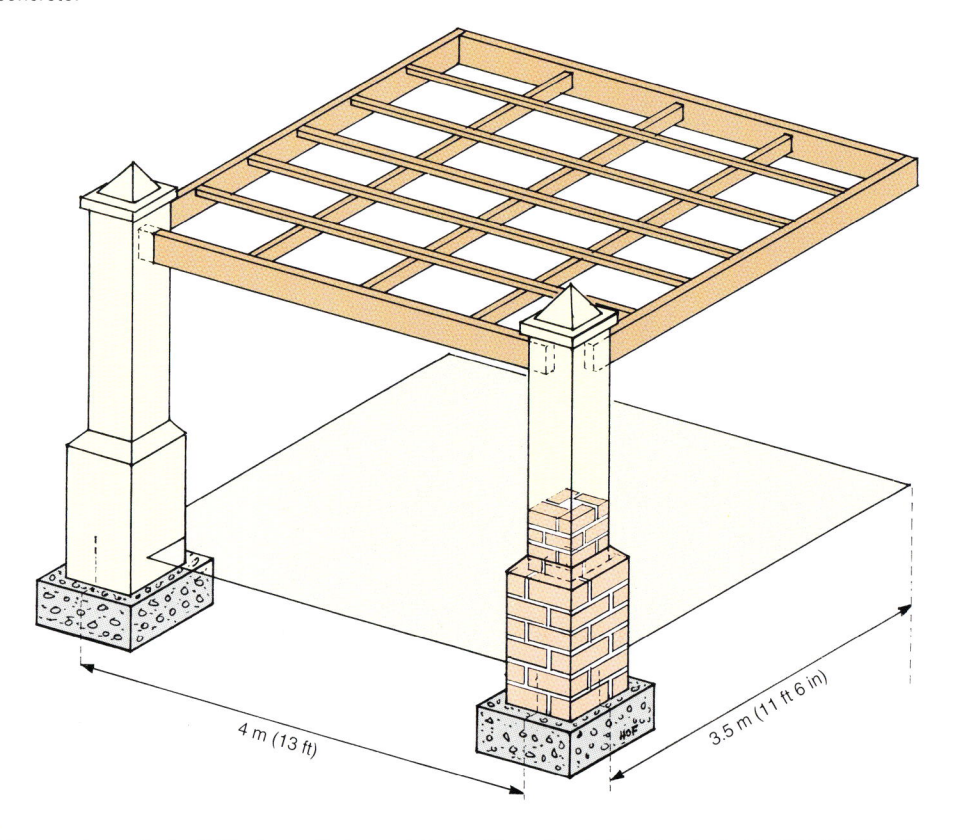

62 BUILD YOUR OWN CARPORT AND PERGOLA

PLAN 12 — GARDEN GAZEBO

This delightful wooden structure houses birdcages in a pretty garden setting. The gazebo could equally provide shelter for seating and alfresco meals. The basic structure was created with poles, while the roof and railings are made of cut and planed wood. The cut-log floor surface adds a rustic feel, although the surface could be paved instead. This project is recommended for people with sound carpentry skills.

MATERIALS

Foundations for poles
115 kg (254 lb) cement
465 kg or 0.35 m³ (1,025 lb or 12 ft³) sand
465 kg or 0.35 m³ (1,025 lb or 12 ft³) stone

Framework
4 x 2.5 m (8 ft) upright poles, 90 mm (3½ in) in diameter
1 x 560 mm (1 ft 10 in) pole for roof, 120 mm (4¾ in) in diameter
6 x 2.1 m x 70 mm x 45 mm (7 ft x 2¾ in x 1¾ in) timber railings
3 x 800 mm x 70 mm x 45 mm (2 ft 7½ in x 2¾ in x 1¾ in) timbers for railing uprights
12 x 1.4 m x 70 mm x 32 mm (4 ft 6 in x 2¾ in x 1¼ in) timbers for railing diagonals
12 x 1.4 m x 32 mm x 22 mm (4 ft 7 in x 1¼ in x 1 in) rafters
8 x 1.7 m x 32 mm x 22 mm (5 ft 7 in x 1¼ in x 1 in) timbers for roof corners
4 x 2.3 m x 32 mm x 22 mm (7 ft 6 in x 1¼ in x 1 in) timbers for roof edges
2 x 3.5 m x 70 mm x 42 mm (11 ft 6 in x 2¾ in x 1½ in) timbers for roof crosspieces
slats to fit 2.6 m² (28 ft²), 70 mm x 10 mm (2¾ in x ⅜ in) in section

Fasteners
wire nails

1 Dig four foundations, 500 mm x 500 mm x 500 mm (1 ft 8 in x 1 ft 8 in x 1 ft 8 in).
2 Set uprights in holes, brace and pour concrete. Allow to set.
3 Buy timber longer than specified and cut to fit. First nail railings to poles (see detail photograph) to strengthen structure, notching timber to fit.
4 Assemble roof structure as illustrated, again notching wood and skew-nailing.
5 Finally nail slats on to fit.

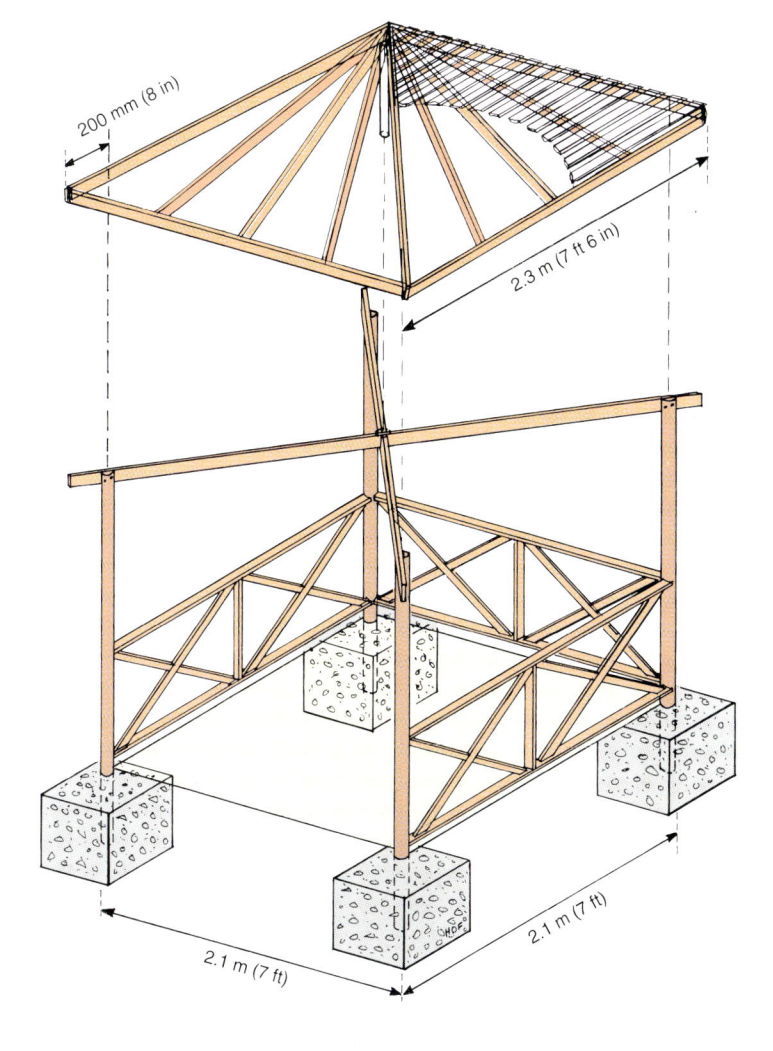

BUILD YOUR OWN CARPORT AND PERGOLA 63

INDEX

Numbers in **bold** refer to step-by-step projects or designs and plans.

A
aluminium 19, 36, **61**
anchorage 30
arbours 6, 15
architect 13
asphalt 16

B
binders 32, 41
bituminous felt 19
brick paving 16, **44-5**, **48**, **51**, **52**, **53**, **54**, **56**, **58**, **60**, **61**, **62**
bricklaying 32-3
bricks and blocks 32, 40-1, **46**, **56**, **57**, **62**
 tools for 32, 38-9
building contractor 13
building regulations 11

C
canvas awnings 19
carports 6-7, **46-7**, **51**, **52**, **53**, **54**, **55**, **56**, **57**
cement 41, see also concrete
climbers and creepers
 see plants
cobbles 16
concrete 16, 29-30, 41, **42-3**, **51**, **55**, **57**, **59**
 precast 35, **53**, **59**
 tools for 38-9
connectors 36

corrugated iron 19, **56**, **57**
costs 12, 40-1
crazy paving 17

D
damp-proof course 24
dimensions 9, 30
decorative elements 26-7
design 14-15
drainage 24
draughtsman 13

E
edging **44**

F
fascia boards 24
fasteners 37
fencing 22
fibrecement 19-20, 36
fibreglass 20, **46**, **52**, **53**, **55**, **57**
flashings 24
floor surfaces 16-18, 24
formwork **42-3**
foundations 29-30
function and needs 8
furniture 27

G
gates 25
gazebos 6, 15, **63**
grass 17
gravel 16-17
ground cover 17
guttering 24, 41

H
hanging baskets 27

L
landscaper 13
laterite 17
latticework 21, 22
levelling 28-9
 tools for 38
lighting 25, 26

M
materials 10-12, 16-25, 29-30, 32, 33, 34, 35-7
 metal 36, 55, see also aluminium, corrugated iron
mortar 32, 41

O
ornaments 27
overhead shelter 19-21, 24, 41

P
paint 19, 33, 35, **51**, **59**, **60**
paving patterns **44**
pebble paving 17
pergolas 6, 15, 31, **48-50**, **51**, **58**, **59**, **60**, **61**, **62**
plans 10, 11
plants 20, 22, 23, 27, **59**, **62**
plastering 33, 41
plasticiser see binders
plumb 29
polycarbonate 20
power tools 40

Q
quantifying 40-1

R
railway sleepers 18
reeds 20

rendering see plastering
roofs see overhead shelter

S
sand 29, 41
screening 22
security 25
setting out 28, 31
 tools for 38
shadecloth 21, **48**, **54**, **58**
shuttering **42**
site 8-10
slate 17, **56**
specialist consultant 13
square 28
stone 17-18, 29, 41
style 9-10, 14
subcontractor 13

T
tarmac 16
tarpaulin 20
thatch 21
tiles 18, 21, **56**
timber 18, 21, 34-5, 41
 cut timber 34, 46, **52**, **54**, **60**, **63**
 poles 34, **48**, **52**, **58**, **63**
 tools for 38-40
tree trunks, sliced 18, **63**
trellises see latticework

V
varnish 35

W
walls 22, 24, **54**, **57**
wood see timber
woodwork 35
 tools for 39-40

USEFUL ADDRESSES

BUILDING CENTRES
Buildex
433 Commissioner Street, Johannesburg
Tel: (011) 618 1252; fax: (011) 614 3818
The Building Centre
209 Cartwrights Corner, Adderley Street, Cape Town
Tel: (021) 461 6095/1121; fax: (021) 461 9265
Natal Master Builders' and Allied Industries' Association Exhibition Centre
40 Essex Terrace, Westville, Natal
Tel: (031) 86 7070; fax: (031) 86 6348

TIMBER
Federated Timber Industries
Head office: Johannesburg Tel: (011) 609 7873; fax: (011) 452 1870
Cape Town Tel: (021) 54 5111; fax: (021) 54 7714
Durban Tel: (031) 42 2011; fax: (031) 42 6958
Bloemfontein Tel: (051) 47 3171; fax: (051) 47 7407
Port Elizabeth Tel: (041) 54 2535; fax: (041) 57 1855
East London Tel: (0431) 43 3733; fax: (0431) 43 5240

BRICKS
Clay Brick Association
Old Pretoria Road, Halfway House
Tel: (011) 805 4206; fax: (011) 315 3966
Concrete Masonry Association
3rd Floor, Flow Systems House, 360 Kent Avenue, Ferndale
Tel: (011) 886 9959; fax: (011) 886 6763

CONCRETE
Concrete Society of Southern Africa/Portland Cement Institute (PCI)
Head office: Portland Park, Halfway House
Tel: (011) 315 0300; fax: (011) 315 0584
Cape Town Tel: (021) 591 5234; fax: (021) 591 3502
Port Elizabeth Tel: (041) 53 2141; fax: (041) 53 3496
Durban Tel: (031) 86 1306/7; fax: (031) 86 7241

OTHER MATERIALS
Alnet (shadecloth)
Head office: Moorsom Avenue, Epping 3, Cape Town
Tel: (021) 54 2321; fax: (021) 54 4003
Johannesburg Tel: (011) 316 2019; fax: (011) 316 3006
Durban Tel: (031) 579 1480; fax: (031) 579 1014
Port Elizabeth Tel: (041) 43 6051; fax: (041) 43 6052
Mitek (connectors)
Head office: 308 Wessels Road, Rivonia
Tel: (011) 803 7540; fax: (011) 803 6999
Durban Tel: (031) 701 0747; fax: (031) 701 0798
Cape Town Tel: (021) 761 6309; fax: (021) 762 2602
Port Elizabeth Tel/fax: (041) 56 2518
Gumbou (connectors)
15 Claybourne Street, Pietermaritzburg
Tel: (0331) 427787
Cottage Castings (period-style poles)
3 Bridgewater Street, Paarden Eiland
Tel: (021) 511 9242; fax: (021) 511 2066